"An overwhelming number of parents are unaware of the long-term importance of what happens during the first three years of their children's lives. This book offers valuable, practical help to parents and caregivers, enabling them to inspire the development of healthy, self-loving children capable of responsibly loving others and contributing to their families and communities."

**—John Vasconcellos, California State Senator,
chair Public Safety Committee**

"This is a deeply encouraging book—full of practical suggestions and based on the principles of respect, kindness, firmness, and encouragement. The suggestions in this book will not make parenting a young child easy (it just isn't); however, they will make parenting a lot more fun."

—Jody McVittie, M.D.

"A practical, well-thought-out guide for a family's first three years."

**—Jane White Vulliet, Program for
Early Parent Support**

"The wisdom in this book is as friendly as yesterday's neighbor, who dispensed the latest tip over the back fence, and more helpful than the advice found in the myriad of other books written to guide today's relationships. *Positive Discipline: The First Three Years* is a foundational blend of research and practical experience upon which to begin stocking your own personalized toolbox with positive, non-punitive tools for building respectful relationships that stand the test of time."

**—Mary Hughes, parent educator and trainer,
mother of three and grandmother of two**

" *Positive Discipline: The First Three Years* gently takes you step-by-step through the simplest and the toughest discipline problems of the early years. . . . There's so much wisdom and common sense here. I wish all new parents were handed the book when they left the hospital room."

**—Rita Golden Gelman, author of
more than 50 children's books**

Positive Discipline: The First Three Years

Also in the
POSITIVE DISCIPLINE Series

Positive Discipline for Preschoolers, Revised 2nd Edition
Jane Nelsen, Cheryl Erwin, and Roslyn Duffy

Positive Discipline for Teenagers, Revised 2nd Edition
Jane Nelsen and Lynn Lott

Positive Discipline A–Z,
Revised and Expanded 2nd Edition
Jane Nelsen, Lynn Lott, and H. Stephen Glenn

Positive Discipline in the Classroom,
Revised 3rd Edition
Jane Nelsen, Lynn Lott, and H. Stephen Glenn

Positive Discipline: A Teacher's A–Z Guide, Revised 2nd Edition
Jane Nelsen, Roslyn Duffy, Linda Escobar, Kate Ortolano,
and Debbie Owen-Sohocki

Positive Discipline for Single Parents,
Revised and Updated 2nd Edition
Jane Nelsen, Cheryl Erwin, and Carol Delzer

Positive Discipline for Your Stepfamily
Jane Nelsen, Cheryl Erwin, and H. Stephen Glenn

Positive Discipline in the Christian Home
Jane Nelsen, Cheryl Erwin, Michael L. Brock, and Mary L. Hughes

Positive Discipline for Childcare Providers
Jane Nelsen and Cheryl Erwin

Jane Nelsen, Cheryl Erwin, and Roslyn Duffy

Positive Discipline

THE FIRST THREE YEARS

From Infant to Toddler—

Laying the Foundation

for Raising a

Capable, Confident Child

THREE RIVERS PRESS • NEW YORK

Published by Three Rivers Press, New York, New York.
Member of the Crown Publishing Group, a division of Random House, Inc.
www.randomhouse.com

THREE RIVERS PRESS and the Tugboat design are registered trademarks of Random House, Inc.

Originally published by Prima Publishing, Roseville, California, in 1998.

All products mentioned in this book are trademarks of their respective companies.

Interior illustrations by Lisa Cooper

Printed in the United States of America

Library of Congress Cataloging-in-Publication Data
Nelsen, Jane.
    Positive discipline : the first three years : from infant to toddler—laying the foundation for raising a capable, confident child / Jane Nelsen, Cheryl Erwin, Roslyn Duffy.
        p.   cm.
    Includes bibliographical references and index.
    1. Discipline of children. 2. Discipline of infants. 3. Infants. 4. Toddlers.
5. Child rearing. 6. Child development. I. Erwin, Cheryl. II. Duffy, Roslyn.
III. Title.
HQ770.4.N437 1998
649'.122—dc21

98-7750
CIP

ISBN 0-7615-1505-4

12 11 10 9

First Edition

*To Rob Reiner, who has passionately dedicated two years of his life
to helping people understand the importance of the first three
years of life through the Reiner Foundation.*
—Jane

. . .

*To all the moms, dads, and babies, to the families they have created—
and to the future we all share.*
—Cheryl

. . .

*For my mom, my own great extended family (related and created),
and all my future grandbabies.*
—Roslyn

CONTENTS

ACKNOWLEDGMENTS

We are often asked, "Where do you get your stories?" We get them from so many people without whom this book could not be written. We owe our biggest thanks to our children. They have provided us with personal family "laboratories." As you will read throughout this book, we believe that mistakes are wonderful opportunities to learn. Our children have put up with many of our mistakes—and have helped us learn from them. We love them, and appreciate them. We have permission to share their stories, they tell us, "as long as we share royalties."

We have had many opportunities to learn from parents in our parenting classes and in our counseling offices. It is easy to "be the expert" with other people. We often tell parents in our classes, "You help me when I get emotionally hooked, and I'll help you when you are emotionally hooked." They often tell us how much we help them. We want them to know how much we have learned from them—and how grateful we are.

We have also had the opportunity to answer questions on *MomsOnline* (*www.momsonline.com*). The questions, and our answers, provided substantial material for this book. We appreciate these moms who are so eager to give their children the love and guidance they need.

We have had excellent editorial help. We gratefully acknowledge Susan Silva, who has worked with us on several books. We can always count on Susan for efficiency and encouragement. When she says she'll do something—she does. And she often takes care of tasks that are beyond the call of duty.

Jennifer Fox has been an excellent editor. She has made several suggestions for better organization and has tirelessly prodded us to take care of important details that could have been missed by less diligent editors.

How can we ever thank Susan Madden enough? Susan is the general manager for Positive Discipline Associates and often put other important tasks on hold while she prepared the manuscript for Prima. She then painstakingly organized all the changes of three authors at each editing stage. And—she gives such good hugs. We can't imagine what we would do without Susan.

We will always be grateful to Alfred Adler and Rudolf Dreikurs, the originators of the philosophy upon which Positive Discipline is based. These psychiatrists left a legacy that has changed the lives of thousands—including us. We feel honored to share these ideas with others.

And oh how we love our families. Instead of complaining about the time it takes for us to write books, they support and encourage us. They constantly demonstrate how capable they are to be self-sufficient instead of demanding. They are proud of us for sharing concepts that have helped us all enjoy each other so much. We love spending every moment we can with them.

PROLOGUE: BY THE CHILDREN

"I AM SERENA. I am three months old. I know my mother's voice and I am really happy when she picks me up. I like to drink my milk. I get really upset when they aren't ready to give me my milk on time. When my mother rocks me to sleep, I like to look around. I like to take my bath but I don't like it when they wash my hair or face. I like it when people talk to me, laugh out loud, and play with me. I want to hold my toys—but I can't. I like to go out everyday because I want to know what is going on. I watch everything."

. . .

"I'M JAMES. I just turned two in December. I want to do everything myself. I don't want any help. I like to do things my own way, even if it takes longer, and if you try to help we have to start all over. If you try putting on my sock, I have to pull it off and do it myself. That is much more important to me than whether I got it on backwards. I keep wishing everybody 'Happy Birthday.' Sometimes I scream. I can't talk too well—I have a hard time getting everything out. But I've learned one word that's *very* powerful: NO!"

. . .

"ME IS BILLY. Me like dinos. Big loud dinos. Move their heads. Rex is meanest. Me eighteen months. Mine Mommy. Mine brother. Me walk. Me drink. Me fast. Me want it now!"

. . .

"I AM JOSE. Next month I will be one year old. I laugh all the time. I like my way. I love to eat. Food is my favorite thing—especially big people's food, but I don't like squash. I am learning to walk. I get a lot of bumps and bruises. I like to chase my cat around the house. Maybe I love him too tight, because he bit my hand yesterday. My favorite words are 'ma-ma,' 'da-da,' 'good,' and 'baby.'"

. . .

"MY NAME IS BONNIE and I am eight months old today. I have two teeth and an older sister. I love to flap my arms when I am happy. I invented a fun game. My mom gives me paper and I eat it up, and then she has to fish it out of my mouth. Then I grin. We play this game with lots of things. We played this game all the time with the pebbles at the beach. Mommy stays real busy searching my mouth. It is fun."

. . .

WE ARE BABIES AND TODDLERS. This book is all about us. Maybe the children you know are like us in some ways. This book takes a peek into our world—or what the world looks like as we lie on tables getting our diapers changed. It's about what we might be thinking when we grab for the shiny things on store shelves, or why we sometimes refuse to go to sleep at night, eat our peas, or use the potty. Learning to understand our world will give you lots of ideas about how to help us grow and how to encourage and teach us. We're newcomers in this world and we need your help all the time. We are lovable, time consuming, and often messy. And there is no one like us in the whole world. This book is for those who love us most.

Positive Discipline: The First Three Years

PART ONE

Welcoming Baby

Learning to Live in Your New Family

The birth of a baby is a momentous occasion, a landmark event that those who have experienced it never forget. We may be shocked by the news that a baby is on the way, or we may be thrilled that the days of pregnancy tests and "trying" finally are behind us. Either way, there is no ignoring this life-changing bit of news. Our lives as independent, spontaneous adults will change: Baby is on the way.

Most adults find that adding an infant to the family, no matter how dearly loved and anticipated, brings changes that take some getting used to. Adult relationships must flex and adapt, making room for the new addition. Schedules and priorities shift; even our bodies change. And babies can be perplexing little people, operating by rules known only to them. The first few months of your new baby's life will be exhausting, exhilarating, and challenging, all at once. No matter how you look at it, life will never be the same!

1

Setting the Stage for Raising Your Child

CLOSE YOUR EYES for just a moment and remember the first time you saw your child's face. That newborn infant may have been red, bald, and wrinkled, but chances are you felt you'd never seen anything more beautiful nor heard anything sweeter than your baby's first cries. Writers and painters have tried to capture the magic of those first moments of life, but words and pictures are rarely powerful enough to convey what happens between parent and child.

For most parents, the months leading up to that miraculous moment of birth are filled with plans, dreams, and a few worries. In reflective moments, we wonder whether we'll be good parents, whether we'll know what to do, whether the baby will be "all right." We talk endlessly about the relative merits of cloth and paper diapers, about nursing or formula feeding. We discuss names for hours, saying them aloud to see how they fit.

We buy and are given impossibly tiny garments and mysterious articles with odd names like "receiving blanket." We wonder if we'll somehow know what to do with them when the time comes. We purchase and ponder over the fascinating gadgetry of babyhood: car seats, swings, carriers, cribs, pacifiers, bottles, breast pumps. Our homes overflow with stuffed animals, mobiles, and hand-knitted blankets and booties. It is a time for endless dreaming, a time for hope and wonder.

Fantasy Versus Reality

SOMETIMES, THOUGH, WHEN we carry that helpless little scrap of humanity home from the hospital, the dreams fade a bit in the harsh light of reality. The baby cries, sometimes for hours without ceasing, and it's up to us to figure out why. The little darling sleeps all day then gurgles happily all night, much to the dismay of his sleep-deprived parents. The baby spits up when we're dressed to go out, has twelve bowel movements in a single night, refuses all known varieties of food, and cries angrily when handed to eager relatives.

From those first moments, parenting young children can become an avalanche of questions, anxieties, and frustrations. The very real love and tenderness remain, but as that precious baby grows, develops, and changes, life becomes an apparently endless stream of new decisions to be made and new ideas to be tested. People look at our beloved child in public places, smile knowingly, and talk about the "terrible twos." Many a young parent feels hopelessly overwhelmed and completely at the mercy of the adorable little tyrant their baby has become.

How Will I Know What to Do?

NONE OF US is born knowing how to be a parent. We learn by watching our own parents and by trial and error. And we worry that those errors may cost more than we can afford. We have so many questions: Do I spank a child or not? If spanking is okay, how soon should I start? How do I get children to listen? How do I communicate with an infant who doesn't understand words? How do I handle a defiant toddler or a discouraged preschooler? How do I decide what's really important? How can I build my children's sense of self-esteem, teach them responsibility and honesty and kindness? How do I get them to share and play nicely? How can I give them the tools to succeed on their own in a difficult and challenging world?

Advice is in plentiful supply—grandparents, uncles and aunts, and the lady behind you in line at the grocery store will have lots of it—but whose advice is right? It is our hope as authors— and as parents—that you will find some of the answers in this book, as well as clues to help you use your own wisdom, creativity, and knowledge of your child (or the children entrusted to your care) to go beyond what can be written in words.

> None of us is born knowing how to be a parent.

This book is designed to be of use to both parents and their frequent partners in child rearing: child caregivers, nannies, and sitters. Examples of home, preschool, and child care situations will be given throughout this book to show how the principles of Positive Discipline can be applied to all aspects of a young child's life. Developmental information will be included wherever appropriate along with recent discoveries about the way babies and young children grow and learn. Because it can be immensely helpful for all the adults who shape a child's life to have the same understanding, you may want to share this book with the people at your child care center, your baby-sitter, or other members of your family.

Your Family Is Your Family

IT CAN HELP to remind yourself that all families, like all children, are different. Not all babies are born into two-parent families with a home in the suburbs, two cars, and a family dog. Your family may indeed look like that, or it may take a different shape altogether. You may be a single parent, through divorce or death or because you never married; you and your partner may have brought children from previous relationships and added those you have together; you may have live-in grandparents or other relatives; or you may share a home with friends and their children.

A family, it has been said, is a circle of people who love each other. Whatever the form your family takes, remember that it will be whatever you have the courage to make it. With wisdom, patience, and love, you can create a place where your children can feel safe, secure, and free to grow and learn and where they can become responsible, respectful, and resourceful people.

The Importance of Long-Range Parenting

LIFE WITH AN active toddler can make us feel like we're aboard a runaway train if we let it. The days rush by, each one filled with new discoveries, new words, new crises. Parents often have to scurry to keep up with their young offspring and sometimes have little time available for thoughtful planning. But think for a moment: Wouldn't it be helpful, as you set out on the journey of parenting, to know your final destination?

Perhaps one of the wisest things you can do right now is to take a moment to ask yourself a very important question: What is it that I really want for my children? When your baby, your toddler, or your preschooler has grown into an adult (as impossible as that may seem now), what qualities and characteristics do you want that adult to have?

You may decide that you want your child to develop responsibility, honesty, compassion, self-reliance, courage, and gratitude—each parent's list will be a little different. What truly matters is this: From your child's earliest moments of life, the decisions you make as a parent will shape his or her future. Each and every action we take—

whether or not we slap our child's hand as she reaches for a delicate object, how we deal with food thrown across the kitchen, or how we respond to bedtime demands—should nurture those qualities we want to encourage.

This thought feels overwhelming to most parents. You may be wondering, "What if I make mistakes? How will I know what to do?" Isn't it wonderful to realize that mistakes are not insurmountable failures but valuable opportunities to learn? Both you and your children will make many mistakes along the way, but they needn't cause irreparable damage if you're willing to learn from them together. The most valuable parenting tools are those you already possess: your love for your child and your own inner wisdom and common sense. Learning to trust them will carry you far along the road to successful parenting.

Remember, too, that children, especially very young children, learn by watching and imitating those around them. Your little one not only will want to push the vacuum or wash the dishes like mom and dad but also will imitate the values you live by, such as honesty, kindness, and justice. Remember that, for children, an action (with both positive and negative results) is a far more effective teacher than a thousand words is. Let your actions as a parent teach your child that he or she is loved and respected, that choices have consequences, and that home is a safe and wonderful place to be.

> Isn't it wonderful to realize that mistakes are not insurmountable failures but valuable opportunities to learn? Both you and your children will make many mistakes along the way, but they needn't cause irreparable damage if you're willing to learn from them together.

A Word About Love

MANY THINGS ARE done to children—or withheld from children— in the name of "love." "I spank my children because I love them," we might say. Or "I rescue and overprotect my children because I love them." "I love my children, so I don't help them much— they need to learn it's a tough world out there." "I push my children—in toilet training, or early reading, or sports activities, or academic excellence—because I love them." "I work long hours because I love my children and I want them to have everything money can buy." "I make decisions for my children because I love them too much to risk letting them make wrong choices." These actions may be done in the name of love, but they are not the best way to show love if you want your children to be responsible, respectful, and resourceful.

Actually, whether we love our children is not the question. The real issue is whether we can show that love in a way that nurtures accountability and self-esteem, a way that helps our children blossom into their full potential as happy, contributing members of society.

How much should we give our children? Is it harmful to let a child have her own way? Should we push our children or let them wander along at their own pace? How much love is enough? How much is too much?

As we will learn in the chapters ahead, children are forming beliefs about themselves and the world around them from their earliest moments of awareness. Parents often say that they feel overcome by the intensity of their love for their children, and it is tempting to demonstrate that love by allowing children to do, say, and have whatever they want. Your eighteen-month-old may be cute and adorable *now* when he grabs the remote control and channel surfs while you're watching your favorite television program. You may even giggle when he tries out the four-letter word he learned at the child care center. Will it still be cute when he's twelve years old and does the same things?

Eventually, most parents realize that true love requires that we love our children enough to teach them, to set wise boundaries, to say no when we must, and to help them learn to live peacefully and respectfully in a world filled with other people. How to do that (and when to begin) is one of the primary goals of this book.

A Word About Dads

THE WORLD OF infants and very young children often seems to be a very female place. After all, giving birth, caring for, and nurturing the very young has traditionally been a woman's job. But times are changing; it is often a child's father who can calm him down, coax a smile, or spoon in the strained peas. We would encourage fathers not to stop with being mere playmates; children can learn so very much from their fathers.

Dads truly are just as good as moms at changing diapers, rocking, singing, bathing, dressing, and teaching—if they choose to be. A young child feels a wonderful sense of belonging and security when both of her parents take an active role in raising her. The world is a busy place, and these days both Mom and Dad are likely to be working—which is all the more reason for parents to share as much as possible in the joys and duties of parenting.

Raising your young child can be more enjoyable and less frustrating when both parents can help each other, share ideas, and work together to solve the inevitable problems. If you are a single mother or father, you can raise a happy, healthy child alone (pick up a copy of *Positive Discipline for Single Parents* to learn more), but if you're lucky enough to be part of a loving parenting team, make the most of it. Your child will benefit from what each of you has to give.

Getting the Help You Need

ALL PARENTS OCCASIONALLY have questions and concerns. Fortunately, parent education and training is finally gaining wide acceptance and credibility. Society has never questioned the need for education and training in occupational fields, be it bricklaying or nursing, but somewhere along the line the notion got planted that parenting should come "naturally" and that attending a parenting class or reading a book on parenting was an admission of inadequacy.

These days, parents are reading books and attending parenting classes in droves, and they testify that what they learn helps them enjoy the important job of parenting as their children learn more self-discipline, responsibility, cooperation, and problem-solving skills.

We highly encourage you to seek out and get involved with a parenting group in your community—or to start one yourself (in your free time, of course!). Reading books and attending classes will not make you a perfect parent—there is no such thing. But you will have more awareness of what works and what doesn't work for the long-range benefit of your children. When you make mistakes, you will know how to correct them—and you will be able to teach your children that mistakes provide wonderful opportunities to learn. (We can't say it often enough!)

Parenting from the Heart

PARENTING GROUPS ARE great places to learn new skills and ideas and to get a little moral support along the way. But when all is said and done, parenting is essentially a matter of the heart and spirit as well as training and knowledge. Perhaps the greatest parenting skill of all is the ability to feel an unbreakable bond of love and warmth for your children and to be able to listen to the voice of love and wisdom even when your patience has been stretched to the breaking point.

No matter how often we say the words, it's all too easy to lose sight of love when we're confronted with the incredible variety of new misbehaviors our children can invent.

The best parenting translates love from words into thoughtful, effective action.

There is a popular children's book by Robert Munsch titled *Love You Forever*. In this little gem, a mother watches her infant sleep and croons to him, "I'll love you forever, I'll like you for always. As long as I'm living, my baby you'll be." As that child grows from baby to terrible toddler to awkward adolescent, the mother creeps into her son's room at night to watch him sleep and to croon that same little song.

The best parenting translates love from words into thoughtful, effective action.

The day comes at last when the mother lies ill and dying, and the son sits by her bedside to sing the old song to her. When he returns home, he shares the song—and the bond of love—with his newborn baby daughter. That feeling—that indescribable tenderness and warmth that a parent feels for a sleeping child—is the heart of parenting.

The next time you tuck your little one in at night, let your gaze rest on that sleeping face; print it firmly in your memory. There are so many things in life that can shake a parent's confidence. We make mistakes; our children make mistakes. We're all learning to be people as we go along, experimenting on each other, blundering occasionally, doing the best we can.

And when you're confronted with a hysterical infant, a defiant toddler, or an angry preschooler—and there will be many such times as the years roll by—close your eyes for just a moment and look in your memory for the face of a sleeping child. Then let that love and tenderness give you the wisdom to deal with the crisis at hand.

Parenting is rarely a simple matter, and no one can challenge or stretch a parent like a very young child who is learning and exploring his world one piece at a time. There will be ample room in the chapters ahead for information, tips, and techniques, but remember that it is always the relationship between parent and child that matters most. If that relationship is based on unconditional love and trust—if your children know from their earliest days that you love them no matter what—you'll probably do just fine. Taking the time now to build the proper foundation by entering your child's world and understanding how he or she feels and thinks and by talking, laughing, playing, and just being together may be the best investment you will ever make in the future of your family.

No one ever said it would be easy to be a parent; it is undoubtedly one of life's most demanding, time-consuming, and unappreciated jobs. But it isn't always easy to be a child these days, either. Have patience; work toward trust and closeness. A little love and understanding coupled with some solid skills and ideas will help you find your way to being the best parent you can be: one who parents from the heart.

Getting to Know Your Child

MARTHA RICHARDS HAD *a story to tell. She collapsed into a chair and waited impatiently for the other members of her parenting group to stop their friendly chatter and settle down.*

The group's leader noticed Martha's exasperation and smiled. "Martha, it looks like you came prepared with something to share. Why don't you start us out?"

Martha sighed and shook her head. "I just don't know what to do," she moaned, the frustration in her voice obvious. "My two-year-old, Daniel, is driving me crazy. He insists on touching things in stores even though I must have told him a dozen times not to touch. He gets angry when I won't read to him or play with him right away—he just can't seem to wait patiently for even five minutes. He's always yanking his hand out of mine when we walk together, and I worry that he'll get away from me or run into the street."

The rest of the group smiled sympathetically and a few heads nodded as Martha told her tale of woe. Other parents had shared such experiences and understood this mom's feelings. "This morning was the last straw, though." Martha paused dramatically, then continued, her voice tight. "This morning Daniel deliberately lied to me. I've told him I won't tolerate lying, but he fibbed right to my face."

The leader met Martha's eyes and nodded. "I can see you're really upset. What did Daniel say?"

"Well," Martha said, "he told me he saw a lion in the backyard. Isn't that ridiculous? There couldn't possibly be a lion in our backyard! And if Daniel starts lying now, what will happen as he grows up?"

Another woman spoke up. "I worry, too. Are the things my child does now signs of how she will turn out as an adult?" Other members of the group nodded.

The concern and confusion these parents are feeling is easy to understand; most parents have similar moments of frustration and disappointment. But there's a good chance that young Daniel isn't intentionally driving his mother to distraction; it's very likely, as Martha's parenting group leader will undoubtedly explain, that Daniel is simply being himself: an active, curious two-year-old who is learning about his world in the only way he knows.

Getting into Your Child's World

ONE OF THE best ways of becoming an effective parent—or, for that matter, an effective human being—is to understand the perceptions of other people, to be able to "get into their world." This is especially true for parents of very young children—after all, their world is so different from ours!

A newborn infant arrives in this world from a place where he's been cradled in warmth and safety beside his mother's heart, his every need immediately met. Suddenly, after a convulsive and tiring journey out of his mother's body, he finds himself in a world of heat and cold, loud noises, moving objects, and bright lights. Faces come and go, voices come from all directions, and this new world runs on a schedule he doesn't yet understand. The instant nourishment and comfort are gone; now he must wail loudly to satisfy his hunger or to find comfort. Sleeping, eating, simply functioning—all must be adapted to the new world. It wouldn't be surprising if we somehow found scientific evidence that infants long to return to the womb!

From the moment of birth onward, a child's early months and years are a voyage of discovery. And one of the first things a child must discover is himself! An infant's control of himself moves from the center outward. At first he is helpless, doing for himself only the most basic bodily functions, unable even to lift his head or to turn over without help.

> From the moment of birth onward, a child's early months and years are a voyage of discovery.

As time passes, his control increases. He learns to really see ("Is that Mom?") and to track objects with his gaze. One day, he realizes that those things that flap in front of his face are his hands and feet; he can make them move, grab them, and even—oh, bliss!—stuff them into his mouth. Later, he learns that he can grab other things with them and stuff those into his mouth as well.

The other developmental milestones follow in due time. A baby learns to turn over, scoot, crawl, pull herself up on the furniture, and eventually walk. Running and getting into mischief come next. Toilet training happens eventually (more about that in chapter 12). The last things to be mastered are the delicate ones, like balance and fine motor control, which explains why a five-year-old or even a six-year-old may have such a difficult time mastering the art of tying shoes. Part of becoming an effective and loving parent or teacher means understanding the world of the little ones you're working with and making every effort to get inside it.

Understanding Your Child's World

IT'S AN OLD question: nature versus nurture, genes versus the environment. What shapes the personality of a human being? Why are our children the people they are? Why is one two-year-old peaceful and compliant, eager to please and easy to get along with, while the two-year-old next door seems bent on challenging every rule, pushing every limit, and breaking everything in sight? We will spend more time discussing these questions in the chapters to follow, but there are a few ideas to keep in mind for now.

Children are a product of their parents' genes (nature), and they are undoubtedly influenced by the environment and ideas around them (nurture). We don't know the exact balance, although recent research appears to indicate that genes play a stronger role than we previously thought. Perhaps it is more important to realize that while children are shaped by both the raw material they inherit and the forces around them, they also bring to the world something uniquely their own: their own spirit, identity, and personality. Have you ever noticed that, despite having the same parents and the same home, children in the same family can be incredibly different? Each of us is unique. Parents need to take time to get to know—and to accept—their children for exactly who they are.

YOUR CHILD'S WORLD

- A child learns about the world by doing.
- A child's frustration due to a lack of abilities or skills may be labeled misbehavior.
- A child's developmental need to explore and experiment may be labeled as misbehavior.
- Young children rarely misbehave purposely.
- A child's physical size and abilities have a strong influence on behavior.
- A child's concepts of reality and fantasy are different from those of an adult.
- Patience is a virtue far beyond the reach of most young children.

Remember Martha and two-year-old Daniel? Let's take a look at some points that might explain the behavior this mom finds so frustrating (we will examine these ideas in more detail in later chapters).

A Child Learns About the World by Doing

A child who is "playing" is actually hard at work, trying on new roles and ideas, tasting, touching, smelling, and experimenting with life. Learning is a hands-on experience filled with the enthusiastic joy of discovery. It takes a while (and some parental patience) before children learn where the boundaries lie.

A Child's Frustration Due to a Lack of Abilities or Skills May Be Labeled As Misbehavior

Parents often expect infants and toddlers to learn abstract concepts that children cannot learn until they are three or four years old or even older. "No" is a good example. We have heard many parents say, "My toddler understands the word 'no' but does it anyway." Children this age do not understand "no" in the way parents think they do. (We will talk more about the word "no" in chapter 14.)

> Parents often expect infants and toddlers to learn abstract concepts that children cannot learn until they are three or four years old or even older.

A Child's Developmental Need to Explore and Experiment May Be Labeled As Misbehavior

Children need secure, loving boundaries in order to feel safe, just as adults need a house with strong walls and a roof to feel protected from the weather, but any self-respecting child will feel obliged to cruise up to the boundaries you've set and test them occasionally, just to make sure they're firmly in place. He's not deliberately trying to drive you insane; he's either exploring at his age-appropriate level or learning about consistency and making sure adults mean what they say (another version of trust). Often adults fail to realize that they simply can't reason with a toddler and spend more time talking than acting. Words, no matter how well we use them, are sounds without real substance to young children. Actions, like removing a child from a forbidden temptation by picking him up and carrying him to another location, provide a clear message. (Some actions, though, only make matters worse: slapping his hand, yelling "no-no," and engaging in a stare-down may invite a child to keep this entertaining adult involved with him—or to retaliate in kind!)

> Often adults fail to realize that they simply can't reason with a toddler and spend more time talking than acting.

Is all of this testing annoying? Of course! Frustrating? Absolutely! But children are rarely as intentionally naughty as their parents think—they're just acting their age.

Young Children Rarely Misbehave Purposely

Adults read motives—that is, intent—into children's behavior all the time. Some act as though their child lies awake at night plotting ways to drive them nuts! Martha's repeated warnings to her son not to touch things aren't terribly effective. Toddlers are highly impulsive little people, and the warnings are simply overpowered by the desire to touch, hold, and explore. A toddler straining over the edge of his stroller to touch a shiny cup on the store shelf does not intend to disobey. The fact that this cup is at the bottom of a highly breakable pyramid of cups has no special meaning for him. The colors on the cup attract his attention; he reaches for it and wants to examine it. He is a mad scientist using his hands, mouth, and imperfect coordination to determine the properties of the marvelous world around him. Our real tasks as parents are prevention, vigilance—and very quick reflexes.

A Child's Physical Size and Abilities Have a Strong Influence on Behavior

Take a moment sometime soon and get down on your child's level. Put your face on the same level as hers—what do you see? The world looks a lot different from down there! Seeing an adult's face requires tilting your head backward—an uncomfortable position if held too long. Most of the time, young children gaze out at a world of knees, shins, and feet, and the only reliable way to catch an adult's attention is to pull on his hands or legs! And just imagine how frightening a yelling, pointing parent would look from down there.

Crib mobiles took on a whole new look when someone had the good sense to look up at what a child was seeing. The cute little animals the adult saw swirling through the air looked like shapeless slivers of moving color when seen from below. Today's versions aim visual images downward.

A child's world shimmers with delightful, distracting images, sounds, and textures. The best way to be sure a tiny person realizes that you are talking to her is to make eye contact. Get down on her level, look into those curious eyes, and speak directly to her.

Are you still down on the floor? If another adult is handy, reach up and take his hand for a moment. Imagine going for a nice long walk through the nearest shopping mall in this position. What parents often believe is defiant yanking away may simply be a child trying to get some circulation back into her hand and arm! In addition, adults have much longer legs than their little ones; children almost always have to run to keep up. No wonder they lag behind us or run away to find their own pace.

> Most of the time, young children gaze out at a world of knees, shins, and feet, and the only reliable way to catch an adult's attention is to pull on his hands or legs! And just imagine how frightening a yelling, pointing parent would look from down there.

It can be frustrating to be a small person whose hands won't quite do the tasks they're expected to. Often children want very much to help, to dress themselves, and to do other tasks around the house, but the sheer mechanics are beyond them. The result is a frustrated, angry child—and a frustrated, angry parent. This does not create a positive atmosphere where learning can take place. How would adults feel if everything they tried was a little beyond their ability to succeed—and they were criticized for the efforts they made? Most would give up and possibly start misbehaving out of sheer frustration. Later we will talk more about expectations, encouragement, and celebrating small steps.

A Child's Concepts of Reality and Fantasy Are Different from That of an Adult

Did you know that when you walk out of your baby's line of sight, you have ceased to exist? That the toy accidentally dropped on the floor has disappeared forever? No wonder babies cry when they are separated from people or things they want—the concept that objects are permanent hasn't developed yet.

In the same way, a young child experiments with his imagination to explore and learn. Our young friend Daniel may not have seen a lion in his backyard, but he may have seen the neighbor's cat. Or he may have watched a cartoon about lions in the jungle. Or his picture book may have included lions and their cubs. Daniel's lion wasn't a "lie," but the product of a vivid imagination and a great deal of curiosity. The line between fantasy and reality remains blurred throughout the first few years of a child's life.

> The line between fantasy and reality remains blurred throughout the first few years of a child's life.

Fantasy may also be a child's way of getting in touch with feelings for which he doesn't yet have words, a way of exploring his own inner being. The lion in the backyard may be another way of expressing a fear of being alone. Careful listening (more about that later) and acceptance by his parents will help him to understand his feelings, learn to sort them out, and find healthy ways of dealing with them.

Patience Is a Virtue Far Beyond the Reach of Most Young Children

Think back for a moment to when you were a child. Remember how long it took for your birthday to come? Have you noticed how quickly the entire process speeded up as you grew older?

Time moves far more slowly for an eager child than it does for an adult. For young Daniel, five minutes may seem like an eternity, and his experience tells him Mom takes far too long to do everything. Yes, children need to learn patience, but parents need to be patient long enough to let them learn. It's not realistic to expect toddlers to sit still for long periods of time—in church or even for story-telling time.

Adults also need to learn that units of time simply don't have the same meaning for children. Jimmy was an extremely bright two-year-old. His parents took him to a drive-in theater one night. It didn't take long before Jimmy was fast asleep—just as his parents had planned. A week later the family drove past the drive-in, and Jimmy said excitedly, "Look, we went there last night!" His father spanked Jimmy for lying. But Jimmy wasn't lying; his father didn't understand child development and didn't realize that Jimmy simply hadn't mastered the concept of time yet. A week, an hour, or last night does not register as different time frames to Jimmy. With more understanding his father would have been delighted at Jimmy's developing memory instead of concerned about his "untruthfulness."

With a little thought and consideration, it isn't hard to see that simply getting into your child's world can provide many solutions to the mysteries of behavior. Your child is a marvelous, unique being. Getting to know children and understanding their perceptions of the world can be an exciting and enjoyable adventure for parents and children alike.

3

Redefining "We"

Living Together As a Family

THE MOMENT YOUR little one finally drifts off to sleep may pose something of a dilemma. Stretching ahead of you are forty-five minutes, an hour, or (if you're really lucky) maybe an hour and a half. What should you do? Lie down and take a nap yourself? Try to make a dent in the laundry pile? Run a hot bath and soak away the tension knotting your shoulders? Few new parents imagined their lives would change this much. New babies bring lots of surprises.

Richard Leski certainly hadn't foreseen moments like this one when his wife first became pregnant. Sometime in the dead of night—his eyes wouldn't focus on the clock's glowing numerals—Richard slowly opened his eyes. It was quiet; what had awakened him? He peered through the darkness of the bedroom and finally saw Gina, his wife, on her hands and knees beside the bed holding a flashlight, tears rolling down her face.

Richard struggled to wake up. "What on earth is wrong, honey?" he said.

Gina turned an anxious face to his. "I had the baby in bed with me and now I can't find him. I thought he might have rolled under the bed."

Richard tried to digest this shocking news. "Gina," he finally said gently, "you know the baby never sleeps with us. I'm sure Brian is in his crib."

Gina blinked slowly at him. "Do you think so? Was I dreaming or something?"

Richard crawled out from under the covers and took his wife's hand. Together they went to look into their three-month-old infant's crib. Brian was sleeping peacefully, one fist jammed into his mouth.

Gina sat down heavily in the rocking chair conveniently placed for night feedings. "I really must be losing it," she said, shaking her head.

Richard smiled. "Gina, the baby wakes up twice a night, every night—you haven't been getting much sleep." But as he led his befuddled wife back to bed and gave her a kiss, Richard wondered whether either of them would survive Brian's infancy. No one had warned them about nights like this!

Raising children—particularly young children—is a demanding, stressful occupation. What other job requires you to be on duty twenty-four hours a day, seven days a week, fifty-two weeks a year? What other occupation requires you to be conversant on child development, childhood illness, and proper parenting techniques, as well as to be an observant supervisor and tireless dispenser of love and nurturing?

New parents soon discover that infants and toddlers require an astonishing amount of time and attention for such small people— yet other demands of life, such as jobs, laundry, and housework, don't go away. Spouses often find there is too little time for each other, let alone the pleasures and hobbies that amused them "B.C." (Before Children). And what happens if other children come along?

One of the most important parts of caring for young children is also one of the most easily overlooked. You have to take care of you. We know; we can hear your incredulous snorts from here: "You've got to be kidding! Where are we supposed to find the time?" That's not an easy question to answer, but it's vitally important to both you and your children that you do. Stress and exhaustion lead to resentment and anger, and parents who feel worn out often overreact to their children's demands and misbehaviors; the result can be words and actions that are deeply regretted later.

> One of the most important parts of caring for young children is also one of the most easily overlooked. You have to take care of you.

Redefining Me, We, and Us

MOST COUPLES DISCOVER that the arrival of a new baby is a moment that transforms their lives forever. Some couples have been together only a short time when the baby arrives, while others have had years to get acquainted with each other and to build a comfortable life. Either way, becoming parents seems to change everything. The transition isn't always as easy and joyful as we would like.

Adding "parent" to your definition of who you are means adding all sorts of new roles and responsibilities. It also means rearranging some of the roles you already have. Most couples find it difficult to be spontaneous with an infant; after all, it's tough to jump up and do something on the spur of the moment when you're lugging diaper bags, infant seats, strollers, bottles, snacks—and a baby. Romantic evenings sometimes go the way of the dinosaur—and so does sex. Household chores that used to be a snap now linger for days, while job responsibilities become difficult to concentrate on. It certainly doesn't help that sleep and serenity may be in short supply!

When we think about it, most of us realize that it takes healthy people to have strong, lasting relationships, to raise a child, and to keep a family together. But when you have young children, remaining healthy and happy takes some work—and some planning. It may be one of the most important parenting tasks you will ever have.

The New Mother's Hairdo

FOR NINE MONTHS, *Susan had watched her body change. In the fifth month of her pregnancy, she began to bid farewell to her belly button. Her size-eight clothes gathered dust at the back of the closet. By month seven, her cheeks resembled a hoarding chipmunk.*

The changes didn't stop there. Thanks to a constricted bladder, Susan knew the location of every public bathroom at the mall. Even her appetite seemed to have a life of its own. Midnight forays to the refrigerator began to resemble feeding frenzies. Her slender, piano-perfect fingers disappeared, to be replaced by little round stubs.

She almost forgot that pregnancy does not last forever. The day finally came when Susan awoke to her own internal earthquake. Powerful muscles propelled her body through hours of labor. Before the sun set, she cradled her new infant daughter to her breast. This tiny creature with fingers barely wider than toothpicks weighed in at just under eight pounds. Everyone gathered round to ooh and aah over this new person.

Not long afterward, Susan faced a fresh crisis. She stepped in front of the mirror a couple of weeks into her new life as a mother and despaired at what she saw. Where was the former, stylish Susan? The chipmunk was only slightly less robust. She shuddered at the thought of donning her stretched-out maternity pants, but size eight remained a distant dream. Who was this stranger in the mirror? What did her husband think when he looked at her changed body? She wanted to be Susan again. Then she lifted her head, straightened her shoulders, and marched to the phone to dial her hairdresser. It was time for a new "do"!

The new mother's hairdo is almost as predictable as labor, delivery, and stretch marks. For months, women experience profound body changes. Bumping into doors, countertops, and people standing in line at the grocery store become common experiences for the expectant mother. The rapid changes of pregnancy make it difficult to remember where her body begins and ends.

The entry of a tiny baby into the world changes forever the way a woman defines herself. The new mother's haircut is an outward symbol of other, inner changes and reflects her need to reestablish a sense of self. Though linked to her new infant on almost every level, a woman experiences a desire to be seen as an autonomous, distinct, and unique person. A new hairstyle is at least a start, virtually screaming to the world, "Look at me! I am a separate person!"

Of course, not every woman gets a new hairdo. But most do find that time is short, and elaborate hairdos—and other bits of personal pampering—take time. Suddenly every spare moment becomes precious. New mothers must reshuffle their priorities. An easy-to-care-for hairstyle means more time for other things, and shorter hair means less for the new baby to grab—a distinct plus. Hair, however, is just the beginning of the changes that lie ahead for the new mother and father.

> When adults can recognize and meet their own needs, children benefit, too.

Longing for your former, more familiar self does not mean you don't love or welcome your child. When adults can recognize and meet their own needs, children benefit, too. It is not just their bodies that parents must seek to reclaim.

From Me to We

ALONG WITH A woman's need to reclaim her sense of self is the need to redefine "family."

Susan spent two years as one half of "Susan and Ed" before becoming pregnant. Becoming a couple had meant quite a bit of adjusting for both Susan and Ed. Susan learned to tuck her blanket in tightly so she wouldn't wake up shivering while Ed snuggled comfortably under both quilts on his side of the bed. Ed had never realized it took so many products to wash one's face. Neither of them anticipated the many unspoken expecta-

tions they brought to their marriage. From serious to trivial, those first two years offered plenty of surprises. Neither of them guessed as they counted days to their delivery date that the surprises had just begun.

Mona loved her single lifestyle. Munching on a carrot might pass for a meal as easily as dining over candlelight with a friend or calling out for pizza. She reveled at the chance Saturday mornings offered for sleeping late. When Mona began to consider adoption, she faced some big choices. Deciding to adopt an infant meant really thinking through her current lifestyle. Once she had made her decision, she energetically tackled all the details. She read everything she could find on parenting, quizzed her friends, bought all the supplies the books recommended, and felt reasonably prepared for the new life ahead. Little did she imagine just how different life would be.

Judith and Frank rejoiced to learn that their family would soon number four. They brought their two-year-old son to the sibling classes at the childbirth clinic. He got to feel his new sister kicking inside his mommy's tummy and he helped pick out a new teddy bear. By the time of Judith's delivery date, they were all prepared for the arrival of family member number four.

Prepared? Well, perhaps not as well as they thought. The reality of life with a new baby is difficult to anticipate. The changes a new baby brings to any household affect every member of it. The redefinition of "we" takes place on every level: physical, emotional, and psychological.

Decorated by Baby

"OVER IN THE *corner, underneath the pile of diapers waiting to be folded, is our sofa.*"

"On the bathroom shelf, right next to the baby tub, sculpted infant sponge, and bag of bath toys, is the box of aromatherapy bath salts my sister gave me last Hanukkah. (Or was it for my birthday? I forget.)"

"Just push aside that baby swing, and I'll clear these bibs and rattles off the chair. Then you'll be able to sit down right here."

Sound a bit chaotic? It usually is. Whatever your house used to look like, baby changed it. A visit to a friend's house used to mean just hopping into the car and driving across town, but now it requires packing the diaper bag, checking for extra changes of clothing, diapers, and teething rings, and carrying the car seat back out to the car, since the baby was sleeping in it when you returned home last night. The simplest tasks become major troop movements.

Just deciding what equipment you need can be overwhelming. How much is too much? Is this a useless gadget or a brilliant innovation? Will our lives be better, easier, or more manageable if we have this item? It's hard to know—so we buy everything. Helpful friends drop off loads of good "stuff" their children have outgrown or throw massive baby showers at which we receive interesting objects whose use we aren't entirely sure of. Before long, every room in the house begins to look like "the baby's room." Those of us who have survived our child's infancy may chuckle, but to an adult who values peace, order, and neatness, this disruption of routine and domestic harmony can be one of the hardest parts of adjusting to parenthood.

Care for Couples: Taking Care of the Two of You

PARENTS WHO ARE contented, healthy, and relatively well rested (being tired seems an unavoidable part of raising young children) are important ingredients in a family that works for all its members. If you are a single parent who must handle it all, there is all the more reason to take special care of yourself. If you have a partner, remember that your relationship is the foundation of your family; invest the time and energy it takes to keep it strong.

It takes time to adjust when a child is added to a marriage or relationship. Before your baby came along, you only had the needs and desires of two people to consider (that's hard enough). Now, suddenly, there are three (or more)—and one requires an extraordinary amount of attention.

Tasks formerly allocated to one parent may need to be redistributed. A new mom caring for an infant, getting less sleep, and struggling with unfamiliar tasks and routines might no longer have the energy to help her partner with mealtime cleanup. A woman who previously did the family laundry might find the need for an afternoon catnap essential to make it through the day ahead; she just can't squeeze in trips to the basement to transfer clothes from the washer to the dryer, collect laundry from bedrooms, or pull clothes out of the dryer to prevent wrinkling. Nursing an infant on demand seems to preclude even the simplest household tasks being done. To ensure everyone's sanity and dignity, it may be time to reassess how tasks are to be distributed. Expectations and standards may need to change, at least temporarily.

Parents can easily lose sight of each other in their headlong rush to "take care of the baby." Mom nurses the baby; Dad feels left out and a little jealous—and guilty for having those feelings. One parent wants a little snuggling and cuddling; the other is "too tired." One parent is dying for dinner and a movie out; the other doesn't trust a baby-sitter or spends the evening phoning home every fifteen minutes to make sure everything is okay. And sex? Baby seems to possess a sixth sense that tells him just when Mom and Dad are contemplating a little intimacy—and that's just when he feels hungry or damp and squalls to alert his frustrated parents!

It is important to remember that your decisions and actions teach your child from her earliest days about life and love and relationships. Taking time for each other isn't selfishness or bad parenting—

it's wisdom. Your child will learn to respect and value the needs and feelings of others by watching you.

Be sure you leave time each week for activities you enjoy, whether it's a special dinner after your child is asleep, a "date" night out, or a morning walk (perhaps with the baby along in a back-pack or a stroller). Couples or parents and older siblings need to take time to really listen to one another and to talk about all the different parts of life, not just the baby! Both parents also need to practice good communication skills. They need to be willing to listen to each other, to speak honestly about their feelings, and to ask for help when they need it during this transition time. It may not seem like it now, but these first weeks and months will pass more quickly than you realize.

> It is important to remember that your decisions and actions teach your child from her earliest days about life and love and relationships. Taking time for each other isn't selfishness or bad parenting—it's wisdom.

More of Us: Making Room for Little Brother or Sister

SOMETIMES BABIES ARRIVE in homes where another child is already in residence—who is not sure he welcomes this intruder. When a new baby is born, relatives, friends, and neighbors arrive to coo over the darling newcomer. The older brother frowns darkly from across the room; he tiptoes over to squeeze the baby's toe when he thinks no one is watching and gets yelled at by Dad. A new baby means older children also must adjust to big changes. "We" used to mean Mom and me, or Mommy, Daddy, and me, or some other combination. Now the definition must stretch to include this unknown (and uninvited) sister or brother.

Parents usually express dismay when older children begin to whine or become uncooperative or boisterous. They insist that the child truly loves his baby brother or sister. That may be true, but the older child sure does miss the spotlight. He needs time to feel special and important to his family while he finds his own way, step by step, toward redefining "we." (See more about birth order in *Positive Discipline* and *Positive Discipline for Preschoolers*.)

Redefining "we" is a process rather than an intellectual activity. An older child who feels sad, a spouse who feels ignored, and a parent who feels lonely for adult companionship are all responding normally to this big change in the family.

One new mom admitted to feeling bored at home all day, since she was used to being surrounded by activity and other adults at her former job. Another described rushing out to the grocery store as soon as her husband got home, just to have an outing and some time to herself. Do not feel ashamed or guilty if you've had the same feelings.

Give each other time to express these feelings without offering judgment, advice, or criticism. Remember, feelings are neither good nor bad, and no one needs to "fix" anyone else's feelings. Create an environment where everyone knows it is safe to express feelings. Venting painful feelings may make room for new feelings of love, joy, and compassion. Remember, too, that feelings can serve as useful prompts to remind us to take care of ourselves. By honoring your own emotions and those of your family, you may discover ways you can solve problems and care for everyone in your family.

Parents Also Have Rights

EVERYONE'S NEEDS ARE important. Struggling with other people's needs tempts us to discount our own. It is important to teach your children to respect your rights and privacy. It may come as something of a revelation to you, but parents also have rights. Remember, respect

SIBLING JEALOUSY

Q. My four-year-old son, Marty, seems to be challenging me and his father more and more since his sister was born five weeks ago. At first he was thrilled to have her, especially because he had always wanted a brother or sister. He has always been an excellent boy at home as well as in child care. He seems to be doing great at child care, but here at home he's always being punished for something or other. He doesn't listen; I can tell him ten times to put on his pajamas before he attempts to make a move to do it (by then I'm mad at him and he gets grounded for not doing what I ask). He has an attitude now and always has something smart to say.

I don't know how to handle this new behavior, and I don't want it to get any worse. I know that the baby takes up a lot of my time, which was time that belonged all to him before, but I can't just ignore the baby. Any advice?

A. Pretend your husband and son have decided that it was so great having a woman like you that they wanted to double their blessings and get another—woman, that is. So in comes the lovely second woman. Because she is new to the household, your husband needs to spend most of his time with her. Since she is trying to get to know everyone, she and your son are always together. In the

should be mutual, and your children will learn best by what they see you do. All of us must learn to respect the needs of others.

Children are, at times, a challenge. They are also one of life's greatest gifts and opportunities. Caring for babies and young children requires tremendous commitment and energy; be sure you make time to refill your own pitcher by taking care of yourself and by remembering to relax and enjoy one another. The hugs and quiet moments of joy will help you get over the bumpy places.

meantime, your husband and son expect you to carry on in your usual lovely way. Instead, you burn dinner. Your husband has to reprimand you and eventually asks you to go up to your room after dinner is over.

Are you starting to get the picture? Do you think you would be more or less likely to burn dinner the next night? They would probably be lucky if you didn't season it with a bit of arsenic!

New babies are hard to take, especially if you're a four-year-old boy who has been an only child his entire life. What your son needs more than grounding and punishment is special time alone with each of his parents. Leave the baby with your husband and go to the movies one afternoon with just your son. If that is too much time to carve out, take him grocery shopping or wash the car together, or simply go for a walk. Your husband and your son also need one-on-one time. Be sure to tell your son how wonderful it is to have someone to do these fun things with and how much you enjoy being alone with him.

Sit down with your son and make a simple agreement about how and when he will do his jobs. You might offer to help him so that you can have some time with him. Right now he is getting any attention he can—even if it is negative. He figures (logically enough) that you love the baby more; after all, look at how much time you spend with this new creature. The way to let him know he still has your love is through actions—namely, spending time with him.

PART TWO

How Children Grow

Learning and the
Stages of Development

Children learn about their own worth and value during their early years. They observe the members of their family and their interactions with one another. They watch their peers and teachers at child care. And they constantly make internal decisions about what it all means. Usually by the age of five a child has decided whether or not she is loved and wanted, whether she's smart or dumb, cute or homely, a joy or a nuisance. These early decisions—some encouraging, some painful—can make impressions that last a lifetime. Your child is always making decisions that will shape his life; the way you treat your child influences the decisions he makes.

Young children can be taught gently and lovingly. They can often understand more than they communicate; they also learn by watching and imitating the behavior of those around them. It helps to remember that the things we *do* are often more influential and powerful than the things we say.

Despite the unique qualities that make your child special and different from every other child, all children pass through a number of developmental stages on their journey to maturity. Learning to recognize and understand these stages will help you make sense of your young child's sometimes challenging behavior and will help you respond in ways that strengthen and encourage your growing child, building a foundation for trust and closeness in the years ahead.

In the next few chapters we will discuss the first three years and the experiences that help or hinder healthy emotional development. We will explain the development of the human brain and describe the formation of trust versus mistrust during the first year of life and the development of autonomy versus doubt and shame that begins in the second year.

4

The Miraculous Brain

How Children Learn

MARTIN AND ROSALIE CHIN *wanted only the best for their baby, Rachel. They spent at least half an hour every day speaking to Rachel while she was still in the womb; they held stereo headphones against Rosalie's bulging abdomen so the baby could learn to appreciate music. When Rachel was born, her proud and ambitious parents brought her home to a nursery equipped with every possible device to speed the learning process. She had special mobiles dancing above her crib; music played constantly; and Martin and Rosalie invested a small fortune in flash cards, "educational" videos, music, and books. They were both intelligent, successful people, they reasoned, and certainly all this early stimulation would help their precious baby make the most of her opportunities in life.*

Jeff and Carol Ennis were also eager to teach. They bought three-year-old Gregory his own watch with a timer, which they set to go off every four hours. When his timer buzzed, Gregory knew it was time to sit down with his mother or father for a lesson. Jeff and Carol coached

Gregory on his alphabet, his numbers, and even computer skills, deter-
mined to teach him to read before he entered kindergarten.

There are many parents like Martin, Rosalie, Jeff, and Carol, loving people doing their best to get their children off to a good start
and help them succeed in school, relationships, and life itself. Until
quite recently, however, we had no way of knowing exactly what
really worked. How do children learn? Are there ways to help them be
more successful and to maximize their potential? Is it wrong to
encourage early learning? What exactly is "success"? Do young children
need academics or social skills? Neither? Or both?

The Living, Growing Brain

WE USED TO believe that babies were born with brains that were
more or less "finished"; all that remained was to fill the waiting brain
with the necessary information. Studies in the past few years have
revolutionized the way we understand the human brain—and, consequently, how babies and children learn about the world around
them. Brain scans and sophisticated imaging techniques have
allowed researchers to peer inside the living brain, to observe its
structure and to discover how it uses energy, blood flow, and special
substances called neurotransmitters to think, to perceive, and to
learn. What those researchers have discovered is extraordinary and
makes it more important than ever before for parents and caregivers
to understand the critical first three years of a child's life.

The human brain begins life as a small cluster of cells in the fetus.
By the fourth week of pregnancy, these cells have begun to sort themselves out according to the function they will one day perform and, to
the wonder of researchers, have begun to "migrate" to the part of the
brain they are destined to occupy. Nature provides the fetus with
more cells than it will need; some do not survive the migration, while
others join together in a network of connections called *synapses*.

This network continues to grow even after the baby is born. By the time a child is two years old, his brain has the same number of synapses as an adult's; by the age of three, he has more than one thousand trillion connections— twice as many as his parents and caregivers! The human brain is "under construction" for the first three years of life, and what a child learns and decides about himself and the world around him becomes part of the "wiring" of his brain. By about the age of ten, a child's brain begins to prune away the synapses that haven't been used enough. By adolescence, half have been discarded.

> The human brain is "under construction" for the first three years of life, and what a child learns and decides about himself and the world around him becomes part of the "wiring" of his brain.

While the brain is amazingly flexible and is able to adapt to change or injury, there are windows early in a child's life during which important learning (like language development) takes place. If those windows are missed, it becomes much more difficult for a child to acquire those abilities. Brain development is a "use it or lose it" proposition—and what is used (and kept) depends on the adults who shape a child's world.

Nature or Nurture?

POPULAR MAGAZINES, BOOKS, and research journals are filled with new studies on human genes and their importance in how we live and who we become. Researchers now believe that genes may have an even stronger influence on temperament and personality than we previously thought; many researchers believe that genes determine such qualities as optimism, depression, aggression, and even whether or not a person is a thrill-seeker—which may be old news to parents who are forever plucking their daring toddlers from the tops of walls, jungle gyms, and trees! Parents may find themselves wondering just how much influence they have on their growing child. If genes are so powerful, does it really matter how we parent our children?

The answer is that it matters a great deal. While a child inherits certain traits and tendencies through her genes, the story of how those traits develop hasn't been written yet. Your child may have arrived on the planet with her own unique temperament, but how you and her other caregivers interact with her will shape the person she becomes (more on temperament in chapter 8). As educational psychologist Jane M. Healy puts it, "Brains shape behavior, and behavior shapes brains."

> It is no longer a question of nature versus nurture: a child's genes and her environment engage in an intimate, complicated dance and both are part of who she will become.

It is no longer a question of nature versus nurture: a child's genes and her environment engage in an intimate, complicated dance and both are part of who she will become. We parents, fragile and imperfect as we are, bear the responsibility for shaping our children's environment. We shape the very structure and wiring of their brains; we shape the people they become and the future they will have.

"Better" Babies

REMEMBER MARTIN AND ROSALIE? They loved little Rachel dearly and wanted to provide her with every opportunity to have a good life. Jeff and Carol, too, wanted only to teach Gregory the things they knew he would need to do well in school. If brains are still growing for the first few years, shouldn't we put in as much information as we can?

The truth is that we don't yet know whether it works to "teach" academics to young children and we don't know the real effect that lots of early stimulation has on their growing brains. Some researchers believe that it may even be harmful to force children to learn too quickly or to absorb concepts that their brains are not yet mature enough to handle. If the brain isn't ready to learn abstract concepts (math, for instance), it may patch together a pathway of connections that is less effective than the one that would have been used later on—and the less effective pathway becomes "wired" in place. There are few absolutes: each human brain is unique and special and it is impossible to generalize about what is right or wrong for an individual child, but some scholars like Jane Healy believe that our fast-paced modern culture (and some of our "educational" television shows) may be affecting children's ability to pay attention, to listen, and to learn later on in life.

Babies and young children learn best in the context of *relationships,* and what they most need to learn in the first three years of life isn't found on flash cards (or on television). How their parents and other caregivers relate to them—how they talk and play and nurture—is by far the most important factor in a baby or toddler's life.

How to Nurture a Growing Brain— and the Child Who Owns It

A YOUNG CHILD'S flexible brain has the ability to adapt to many different environments and situations. What he learns in his first years determines which connections the brain will keep—and which will be lost. Children who grow up with abuse or neglect may forever lose the ability to trust and may decide early in life that they have little value. On the other hand, children whose early experiences are happy and healthy will build into their growing brains qualities and perceptions that will help them thrive.

Many of the recommendations experts now make are steps wise parents have taken instinctively from the beginning of time. When we understand the true importance of these ways of nurturing a baby, however, we can do them consciously and know that we are providing exactly what our young children most need from us.

What should parents know? What can we do to give our children healthy brains—and healthy lives?

Respond to Your Baby's Cues

Responding when a baby cries, providing food, a clean diaper, or a snuggle, is important in helping that baby learn trust, one of the most vital early lessons. Parents also can learn to recognize when a baby needs quiet time to nap or just to be still; they can respond to an infant's kicking legs and waving fists, smiling back or playing finger games when he is eager for stimulation.

Your baby will let you know his preferences, what he needs and when, and the more time you spend with him the easier it will

ENCOURAGE YOUR BABY'S BRAIN DEVELOPMENT

- Respond to your baby's cues.
- Touch, speak, and sing.
- Provide opportunities to play—and play along.
- Encourage curiosity and safe exploration.
- Allow private time for your baby.
- Use discipline to teach—never shake or hit.
- Take care of yourself.
- Select child care carefully.
- Love and enjoy your child.

become to recognize his signals. There is simply no substitute for time and attention, and children who have the opportunity to bond well with parents find it easier to get along with others and to be comfortable in their world as they grow up.

Touch, Speak, and Sing

Studies have shown that babies who are touched, massaged, and held often are less irritable and gain weight more quickly. Holding, rocking, and cuddling a child communicates love and acceptance perhaps better than anything else. Babies, toddlers, even parents need hugs, and a loving hug may be all the "help" your little one needs for many of life's small crises.

Many adults are not comfortable with physical touch. Many weren't hugged or touched themselves, or perhaps the touching happened in the wrong way. Fathers, especially, can feel uncomfortable touching or hugging their children and sometimes substitute roughhousing and wrestling (which can be lots of fun) for snuggling and affection. While touch should *always* happen in the right way and at the right time (even toddlers can be taught about "good touch" and "bad touch" in ways that won't frighten them), touch helps your little one attach to you and provides both comfort and stimulation. As children grow, a pat on the shoulder or a wordless hug may communicate more than the most eloquent speech.

> Studies have shown that babies who are touched, massaged, and held often are less irritable and gain weight more quickly.

Speaking, too, is important. What grown-up can resist cooing gentle words to a newborn? Talking and reading to infants and young children who obviously can't yet understand your words may not seem important, but these "conversations" stimulate the parts of a child's brain responsible for speech and language development (more on language and feelings in chapter 16). Remember that while repetition may be boring to you, it isn't to your child. Babies and toddlers learn through repetition. You may think you cannot endure *Pat the Bunny* one more time—but your little one will remain delighted with the sounds and touchable textures of this old favorite for months. Knowing that you are shaping a healthy brain may give you the patience it takes to tell favorite stories over and over again. Incidentally, television does not have the same effect on babies and toddlers as real speech. Television is not conversation, and its frantic, flashy structure may actually negatively affect a child's attention span and ability to listen. There is no substitute for *talking* to your child and no better way for her to learn.

Music also appears to have a powerful influence on growing brains. While little Megan may not care whether it's Mozart or "Silly Songs" she hears, the melody and rhythm will affect her. Music seems to stimulate creativity; our hearts and brain waves tend to speed up and slow down to match the pace of the music we're listening to. There can be few things as delightful as watching a dancing toddler, spinning and bouncing to the strains of a lively tune or one of Dad's old rock 'n roll favorites. Don't rely only on recorded music, either: sing to your young child (yes, you *can* sing— your toddler isn't a critic!). At first, you will sing nursery rhymes and songs, lullabies, or a favorite from a child's recording alone, but before long your toddler will be yodeling along. It isn't noise: it's the sound of healthy brains growing!

> Television does not have the same effect on babies and toddlers as real speech. Television is not conversation, and its frantic, flashy structure may actually negatively affect a child's attention span and ability to listen. There is no substitute for *talking* to your child and no better way for her to learn.

Provide Opportunities to Play—and Play Along

In these days of busy parents and overburdened caregivers, confinement in infant seats and playpens and time spent in front of a video or television show often substitute for play. But babies and toddlers are just discovering their bodies—and just forming the vital connections that link brain with action. They are developing their motor control and learning about textures and gravity. They need the opportunity to play actively.

Play truly is a child's work. It is how she experiences her world, learns about relationships, and tries on new roles and personalities. Parents are usually good at taking children places where they can play—we're endlessly on the road to gymnastics, "water babies," or play group—but we're often less good at playing ourselves. There is no better way to understand your toddler's world than to play with him.

Computer games and sophisticated toys may be fine, but they may be so fancy that they hamper a child's active creativity. Children can play with—and learn from—the box the toy comes in or the pots and pans under the sink. The old-fashioned, interactive favorites still serve a valuable purpose; provide building blocks, dress-up clothes, a sandbox, and lumps of clay, then watch as your little one discovers the joy of building, touching, and shaping his world. Better yet, play *with* him. Get down on the floor and build a fort out of sofa cushions, or play a favorite board game (older toddlers love Chutes and Ladders or Candyland and can play well with only a little help from you); have a water fight or play in the mud. You'll be creating special memories and a bond with your child that both of you will treasure, and you will also be giving him opportunities to build vital connections in his growing brain.

> Computer games and sophisticated toys may be fine, but they may be so fancy that they hamper a child's active creativity. Children can play with—and learn from—the box the toy comes in or the pots and pans under the sink.

Encourage Curiosity and Safe Exploration

Again, infant seats, baby swings, and playpens may be a necessity from time to time, but your active toddler needs time and space to work on her sense of autonomy and initiative, and there's no better way than being allowed to roam and explore the house, the yard, or the neighborhood park—with your supervision, of course. (See chapters 6 and 7 for more on autonomy—and childproofing.)

Research has shown that a child's brain grows and is stimulated best by things that she is actively interested in. If your little one shows curiosity about colors and paints, animals, or big trucks, you'll be helping her brain develop by finding ways to explore what she most wants to learn about. You aren't pushing a three-year-old to read if she initiates the process—and a few do. On the other hand, pressuring a little one to read by placing flash cards on every item in the house is a waste of time at best; most children would prefer to explore every item instead of reading it. At worst, this sort of pressure can create feelings of inadequacy in a child who senses your disappointment in his failure to acquire scholarly accomplishments. Each human being is unique and fascinating; take time to discover what makes your little one sparkle, then create opportunities to explore.

Allow Private Time for Your Baby

Please don't get the impression that your baby needs constant stimulation. Babies need private time to explore by themselves. When you see an infant staring at his fingers or playing with his toes, he is exploring. Many babies are very content to sit in their infant seats and follow you with their eyes as you occupy yourself in other tasks.

As usual, we come back to balance. It is good to provide stimulation—talking, cooing, and singing—but not all the time. Overstimulation can actually make a baby crabby, and too much stimulation can be counterproductive for optimal brain development. In his book *The Self-Calmed Baby,* William Sammons points out that "The ability to self-entertain is one of the most important skills children can develop." Babies can also learn to fall asleep by themselves (an issue discussed more thoroughly in chapter 10).

Use Discipline to Teach—Never Shake or Hit

Growing brains are fragile miracles. Every day an infant dies or is permanently disabled by being shaken or hit by an angry, frustrated adult. "I would *never* hurt my baby," you may be saying, but it may come as a surprise to you to learn that harsh criticism, punishment, or shaming may also damage a child's brain. Remember, those connections that are used most will become permanent; those not used will be lost forever. All parents make mistakes, and all parents will experience the intense frustration and exhaustion that happen sometimes when we share our lives with very young children. When we are aware of the long-range effect of the way we treat our children, we can make choices that will not only teach and provide the structure children need but allow them to learn that they do belong and have significance—lessons that will last a lifetime.

> "I would *never* hurt my baby," you may be saying, but it may come as a surprise to you to learn that harsh criticism, punishment, or shaming may also change a child's brain.

This book is filled with ways to practice Positive Discipline, which teaches the skills to balance kindness with firmness. Isn't it good to know that you are not only helping your child behave more appropriately but also nurturing his growing brain?

Take Care of Yourself

How, you may be wondering, does my health and state of mind affect my child's brain? Parents and caregivers are the most important people in a young child's life. The quality of what we have to offer is often affected by our own all-too-human moods and emotions. Stress, exhaustion, or worry affect the way we interact with babies and toddlers—and, consequently, the way they perceive us and themselves.

A mother's depression and exhaustion may not invite much more than fussiness during the first six months of life; nature seems to have taken into account the topsy-turvy emotions that commonly follow the birth of a baby. But if Mom's depression continues into an infant's first eighteen months, it can have a much greater impact on her child. Depressed or exhausted mothers are less responsive to infants, which affects what those infants are learning about their world. Interestingly enough, when depressed mothers seek treatment and begin to recover, their babies' brain activity returns to normal.

In chapter 18, we will take a closer look at the importance of care and nurturing for those essential people, the parents. For now, realize that your little one depends entirely on you. Taking care of yourself isn't selfishness; it is wisdom.

Select Child Care Carefully

A child's growing brain does not shut off when he is dropped off at the child care center. Many parents must work outside the home these days, and many babies and toddlers spend the bulk of their waking hours in a child care facility. The same qualities that are essential for parents in nurturing developing brains are just as critical for child care providers; unfortunately, the same research study that presented much of the new brain research states soberly that as many as 40 percent of infants and toddlers are in child care arrangements

that jeopardize their development. We will look more closely at child care, particularly how to select care for your child that promotes her safety and development, in chapter 17. On the other hand, brain development may be enhanced through the appropriate stimulation provided in quality child care.

In the best of worlds, parents and caregivers work together to nurture developing brains, consistently providing the time, attention, conversation, and balance of freedom and structure that young children need. Time spent choosing a child care provider is time invested in the long-range health and happiness of your child.

Love and Enjoy Your Child

Yes, it works here, too. Remember, what children (and all of us) need to know is that we belong, that we have a special place in life, and that we have value to those around us. No matter how busy your life and no matter how seriously you take your responsibilities as a parent, take time to simply love and enjoy your child. The quiet moments of wonder, the laughter and giggling, the delight we take in the special qualities, first words, and adorable actions of these new little people are not wasted time but precious investments in the future of your family. The housecleaning, yard work, and laundry will wait; slow down occasionally and just enjoy the time you have with your child. It speeds by all too quickly.

> No matter how busy your life and no matter how seriously you take your responsibilities as a parent, take time to simply love and enjoy your child.

The First Three Years Last Forever

BY NOW YOU may be feeling more than a little concerned. So much is happening in the first three years of a child's life; conscientious, loving parents frequently worry that they won't be able to meet their child's needs, that they will leave some task undone or fail to provide the care and environment that their child's growing brain requires. It may help a bit to remember that none of us is perfect—and we don't need to be. Your baby or toddler doesn't require perfection; he only needs you to be warm, loving, and aware of his needs.

The Positive Discipline approach to raising young children fits well with our new knowledge of how the human brain develops, and doing your best will almost certainly be "good enough." Awareness is always the first step to action, and knowledge will help you make choices and decisions that are in the best interest of your baby or toddler. (For more information on the new brain research and your child's first three years, contact the Families and Work Institute, 330 Seventh Avenue, 14th Floor, New York, NY 10001, 212-465-2044, or the Reiner Foundation at "I Am Your Child," *www.iamyourchild.org.*)

Raising a young child is indeed a serious responsibility. In many ways, a child's first three years last for the rest of his life.

5

Trust Versus Mistrust

"Can I Count on You?"

A SENSE OF TRUST means that an infant feels or senses that she can rely on the affections and support of others. To develop a sense of trust during the first year of life, a baby needs to have his or her basic needs met consistently and lovingly. These needs include proper nutrition, a comfortable temperature, dry diapers, adequate sleep, and lots and lots of touching, holding, and cuddling. Many parents feel confused about the difference between meeting their babies' needs and spoiling—and they're sure to hear many points of view (some welcome, some not).

Opinions range from "put your baby on a strict schedule (after all, he or she has come to live in your house and there is no reason to change your life too much)" to "forget about your life; hover around your baby and try to anticipate every need and whimper." Understanding the importance of your child developing trust instead of mistrust is a key factor in deciding what is right for you and your baby.

A neglected baby (one whose basic needs for food, comfort, and loving touch are not met) will develop a sense of mistrust in life.

Perhaps surprisingly, an extremely pampered baby may also develop a sense of mistrust because he has never had to learn patience and self-reliance. Many new parents are plagued with guilt if they don't devote twenty-four hours a day to their new baby.

Help! I'm a Slave to My Baby: Understanding "Developmental Appropriateness" in the First Year of Life

PART OF UNDERSTANDING and managing young children's behavior involves knowing what is "developmentally appropriate," a term we use to describe the characteristics and behaviors that are expected for children at certain ages (as discussed more thoroughly in chapter 9). The more we know about the psychological, intellectual, and physical development of the child, the more we know what is

TRUST VERSUS MISTRUST

During the first year of life, a child begins to learn the fundamental concept of trust, the first important stage of emotional development. If she cries, does someone come? If she's hungry, cold, or wet, will someone help? Do the routines and rituals of daily life happen predictably? It is by these simple experiences that she will learn to trust and rely on her parents.

Without this basic trust, life becomes far more difficult. Children who have been shuttled in and out of foster homes during their early years or who have been denied affection and consistent care often refuse to make eye contact or to respond to even the most loving attempts later on. It can take a great deal of

developmentally appropriate and the better our ability to get into our child's world and shape his behavior. An understanding of developmental appropriateness helps us know that it is almost impossible to spoil an infant.

Spoiling

DON'T WORRY ABOUT spoiling your baby during the first three months of life. It can happen, but it is very rare.

Sylvia managed to spoil her infant because she hardly ever put him down. She held him as she puttered around the house; she held him as she fixed the meals; she even held him after he had gone to sleep. By the time her baby was two months old, he screamed every time Sylvia tried to put him down. There was no escape even when he slept; if she tried to lay him down, he would wake up and scream.

This example provides a good definition of spoiling—when the child becomes demanding and the parent feels like a slave to the

patience and determination to build in these children the willingness to trust that was stunted during their early years.

Most of us know people who have a hard time trusting themselves or others and who seem to have little faith in their ability to influence what happens to them. Will your child go through life with an attitude of trust or mistrust, faith or doubt? It all depends on how he is treated in the first year of life (and the subconscious decisions he makes about his experiences), according to psychologist and human development expert Erik Erikson. This critical first year of life is also the first stage of emotional development. Although the development of trust begins in the first year, it is an ongoing process, as are all of the stages of emotional development.

child. Babies need to have their cries responded to, at least initially (this teaches trust more effectively than anything else), but considering your baby's needs, your own needs, and the needs of other members of your family will help you introduce routines and begin to find a good balance. Sometimes crying may be a child's way of saying, "I don't like this." However, that doesn't mean he can't deal with it. This is an important concept to master, and we will learn more about it in the chapters ahead.

If you feel at the mercy of your three-month-old baby's demands to be held, pick her up for just a few minutes, cuddle and coo, and then place her in a playpen with a musical mobile, or place her in a safe infant seat where she can watch what you are doing. The key is a balance that meets the needs of everyone concerned. A baby should not be left in a playpen or infant seat too long, and a parent should not feel like a slave to his or her child.

> The key is a balance that meets the needs of everyone concerned. A baby should not be left in a playpen or infant seat too long, and a parent should not feel like a slave to his or her child.

Learning the difference between what an infant truly *needs* and what he simply *wants* causes considerable anxiety for parents, but as your understanding increases so will your confidence. We need to use our heads and our hearts to be effective parents. The more information we have, the more we can trust our heads. The more we know how important it is to enjoy our children, the more we can trust our hearts. When in doubt, always trust your heart.

Uniqueness, Self-Trust, and Parent Confidence

TO SAY THAT people are different and unique isn't new or profound, but it doesn't hurt to be reminded. Because parents are unique, they will be comfortable with different methods of parenting. We must also remember that children don't all respond in the same ways.

What does all this have to do with the development of trust or mistrust? Erikson found that a primary factor in the development of a child's trust is her sense that her primary caretaker—usually her mother—has confidence in herself.

Because self-confidence is so important, we want to repeat that most mothers find they can trust themselves more when they have a basic understanding of child development and parenting skills—and faith in their own instincts. This is one reason why parent education can be so important. When you have learned all you can about child development, age-appropriate behavior, the mistaken goals of "misbehavior," and nonpunitive methods to help your child thrive, the easier it will be to feel secure in your ability to understand and care for your child.

> The more information we have, the more we can trust our heads. The more we know how important it is to enjoy our children, the more we can trust our hearts. When in doubt, always trust your heart.

Children do develop trust when someone comes when they cry, but many parents misinterpret this to mean that their child will be traumatized if they don't respond to every whimper. By pampering and coddling, they fail to help a child develop courage and self-confidence. For example, after a child has been fed, changed, and cuddled, she might whimper (or even cry) for a few minutes after being put into her crib. She hasn't yet had the opportunity to learn that she is capable of falling asleep by herself.

When parents think they have to help their children get to sleep by rocking them, nursing them or giving them a bottle, or even lying down with them, their children may be learning manipulation skills instead of trust (in themselves and in their parents).

It takes knowledge and confidence (and faith in your child) to know when it is okay to allow your child to experience a little discomfort in order to develop trust and confidence in herself. Remember that no parent is born knowing where this balance lies—

and mistakes are opportunities to learn. Pay attention not only to your baby but to your own feelings and wisdom, and chances are good that you'll soon know what works for your special child.

Enjoy Your Children and Yourself

DOES THIS REALLY need to be said? We think so. We all have been confused and overwhelmed by the responsibility of parenting. Sharing your life with a child, especially during his first year of life, can be an overwhelming experience. Everything is new; the baby is demanding, and we all have moments when we worry if we're doing it "right."

Whenever you feel that way, just forget everything else and remember to enjoy. When you forget to enjoy, learning new skills and adjusting to life with a developing child can seem like a heavy burden. Your baby will sense your worry and doubt and his growing sense of trust may be hindered. When built on the foundation of

HELP YOUR INFANT DEVELOP TRUST

- Meet basic needs (know the difference between needs and wants).
- Avoid pampering (have faith in children to handle not receiving all wants).
- Learn about developmental needs (social, intellectual, and physical).
- Learn parenting skills (including long-range results of what you do).
- Have confidence and trust in yourself.

enjoyment, awareness, and education, confidence will filter through your heart and you will know what to do (yes, you really will!).

Making Enjoyment a Priority

WHEN YOU HAVE small children, you may as well forget about being a perfect housekeeper, running the PTA, or taking on anything that makes you feel stressed and robs you of time to enjoy your children. Discuss priorities with your spouse and make an agreement to put first things first—each other and your children. Agree to be satisfied with soup and sandwiches for a while instead of elaborate meals.

Why is this important? Isn't it possible to "do it all"? It may be; but keep in mind that infants can sense the energy of their parents. They often become fussy when their parents are upset. They also sense when you enjoy them—and know when you don't. How can infants develop a sense of trust if they don't feel the energy of enjoyment from their parents and know that they are loved, wanted, and appreciated? (We will explore communication and love further in chapter 16.)

Ask yourself this question when circumstances get in the way of simply enjoying your children: "What difference will this make ten years from now?" Whether or not the house is clean, the lawn is mowed, or the furniture is waxed won't make any difference; on the other hand, time you spend with your spouse and your children will make all the difference in the world!

6

Autonomy Versus Doubt and Shame

"I Can Stand on My Own Two Feet (but Don't Abandon Me!)"

WHAT DO TODDLERS want to do? Just about everything: explore, touch, examine, put their fingers in sockets, play with the television knobs, empty cupboards of every pot and pan, play in the toilet, unravel the toilet paper, eat lipstick, spill perfume, and investigate everything they can get their hands on.

What happens when parents don't allow toddlers to explore? What happens when parents slap their children's hands when they touch something they are not supposed to touch? Well-meaning parents who have not learned about this important developmental phase may not know that too much confinement and punishment can instill doubt and shame instead of a sense of autonomy. Notice that we said a *sense of* autonomy—not autonomy itself. Erik Erikson, a psychologist and human development expert, used the words "sense of" to describe a leaning in one direction or the other. It is impossible for children to develop full autonomy. However, parents can facilitate their inclination toward the development of autonomy versus doubt and shame.

In the first year of their lives, we must help children develop a sense of trust rather than mistrust. Erikson believed that between the ages of one and three, children have the opportunity to begin their quest for a sense of autonomy that is stronger than feelings of doubt and shame. This search for a sense of autonomy continues throughout childhood, but the foundation is established in the second and third years. A strong sense of trust developed in the first year and a strong sense of autonomy developed in the second and third years also build the foundation for healthy self-esteem.

What Is Autonomy?

SINCE A STRONG sense of autonomy is so important, we need to know what it is and how to help toddlers develop it. The dictionary defines "autonomy" as independence or freedom, having the will of one's actions. "What?" you might ask. "Give my toddler independence and freedom? My toddler is still a baby who needs to be dependent on me!" A toddler needs both autonomy and healthy dependence on you. He needs a balance between the security provided by parents and home and the freedom to discover his own capabilities.

This is illustrated beautifully by the research of Harry F. Harlow using monkeys and their young. In his study, the mother monkeys took their babies into a room full of toys. The baby monkeys clung to their mothers while they surveyed the interesting toys in the room. Eventually, their need to explore took over, and they left their mothers to play with the toys. Periodically, they would return and jump into their mothers' arms for another dose of security before going back to their play. Children are not monkeys, but they too

Well-meaning parents who have not learned about this important developmental phase may not know that too much confinement and punishment can instill doubt and shame instead of a sense of autonomy.

AUTONOMY VERSUS DOUBT AND SHAME

The second stage of emotional development, which begins during the second year of life, determines whether your child will go through life with faith in his autonomy (self-control and self-confidence) or will struggle with feelings of doubt and shame. The frustrations we all encounter in life often create thoughts of doubt and shame within us; however, psychologist and human development expert Erik Erikson believed that our experiences during the second year of life are especially crucial to developing a sense of autonomy that is stronger than the thoughts of doubt and shame.

need a gentle blending of safety and freedom. Too much freedom, however, could be very dangerous and threatening for a toddler.

It is easy to misunderstand what autonomy means for a toddler. Possessing autonomy does not mean that children no longer need guidance and safe boundaries. They do. They also need a lot of freedom within those safe boundaries so they can begin that important journey toward independence—and, eventually, interdependence.

Autonomy does not mean that children are prepared to make decisions about life situations. Asking a child whether he wants to hold the keys or your purse gives him a healthy opportunity to experience his own power. Asking him whether he would prefer this preschool or that one, whether the family should visit Grandma's at Thanksgiving, or whether he would mind if Mommy and Daddy go to a movie tonight may teach him that he must be in charge. Such decisions are adult responsibilities. Burdening children with too many choices—or the wrong sort of choices—creates demanding, anxious tyrants.

When children come into the world, they are totally dependent. Parents are most effective when they help their children learn the skills of independence (autonomy) and interdependence. Healthy independence is the foundation for healthy interdependence. *Positive Discipline for Parenting in Recovery* offers an excellent description of independence:

Many people have the mistaken idea that being an independent person means not needing anyone. . . . This idea is unfounded. Independence means people know what they think, what they feel, and what they want. It means they have skills to express what they think and feel to others in a respectful manner. It means they have the skills to accomplish what they want most of the time, sometimes by themselves and sometimes with others. Only when members become independent and express their uniqueness can they break the codependent patterns and move toward interdependence.

With awareness, parents can avoid the mistake of creating a codependent relationship with their children—in the name of love.

With awareness, parents can avoid the mistake of creating a codependent relationship with their children—in the name of love.

I Am Me, You Are You, and We Can Be Together

POSITIVE DISCIPLINE FOR PARENTS IN RECOVERY offers this explanation of interdependence:

Picture two people leaning on each other for support. If one moves, the other falls. This is codependence. Now picture those same two people near each other and available to help and connect, but with lives of their own and skills of their own. There is a lot of give and take through respect and support for individual differences. This is interdependence.

Most people fantasize about interdependence when they think about building a relationship or a family. Then, without realizing it, they sabotage interdependence when their fears (or lack of information about effective parenting skills) keep them holding on and refusing to let go.

The process of developing interdependence begins at birth, as parents gradually "let go" as their children grow and begin to develop new skills and the confidence to use them. The first time a mother disappears from her child's side and then reappears nurtures the beginning tendrils of trust. Cuddling, feeding, soothing, and playing with a baby reassures her about the world she has entered. Supported by growing trust, a child begins to learn to soothe herself. Thus baby steps toward autonomy begin. Growth toward independence and interdependence is a lifelong process that will be much easier for children who develop a strong sense of autonomy during their second and third years.

Toddlers can only develop a sense of autonomy, not complete independence. Not only is complete independence at this age impossible, but allowing too much independence would be permissive parenting. And permissive parenting is not effective parenting.

Encouraging Autonomy Does Not Mean Being Permissive

AS WE HAVE SAID, autonomy does not mean children should be allowed to do anything they want. One of the more persistent debates about parenting in early childhood concerns childproofing a home: removing poisons, plugging electrical sockets, latching kitchen cabinets, putting valuable or fragile items out of reach of young hands, and otherwise making the home environment safe for a child to explore. The importance of developing a child's autonomy is an excellent argument in favor of childproofing your home. Some adults fret that childproofing fails to teach children about restraint. However, developmentally, young children are programmed to explore. When we ignore developmental needs, then stress will result, and conflict and power struggles rarely teach anyone anything. Once the home is childproofed, there will still be many things children should not be allowed to do, such as climb on the furniture.

Some parents believe the best way to teach toddlers not to touch things or do what they shouldn't is to slap their hands. Think for just a moment. Toddlers would not be normal if they didn't want to explore and touch. They're doing their developmental job, and it is an important ingredient in their sense of autonomy. Does it make sense to slap or spank them for doing something that is normal and important for healthy development? Slapping and spanking, especially for something that is a part of normal development, is far more likely to create a sense of doubt and shame than healthy autonomy. Removing a child from a forbidden or dangerous item allows the needs of both the child and the situation to be met respectfully. (We'll learn more about distraction and other positive discipline tools later on.) Effective parenting can help children learn limits without creating doubt and shame. It requires kindness and firmness at the same time.

> Effective parenting can help children learn limits without creating doubt and shame. It requires kindness and firmness at the same time.

Encouraging a Sense of Autonomy

IMAGINE AWAKING FROM a deep sleep and discovering that you are in an unfamiliar new world and must learn not only how your own, brand-new body and emotions work but how the people around you live—and what they expect from you. Learning to survive and thrive would require a great deal of courage.

Just being a toddler takes courage. A young child's budding sense of autonomy gives him the courage and energy to set about exploring how this world works. It's a task fraught with perils—for toddlers and for parents. Healthy autonomy is a balance between protecting children and allowing them to explore and test the world they will inhabit. How much is too much? How will we know when we (and our children) have the balance right?

The Need to Explore in a Safe Environment

AN IMPORTANT PART of the development of autonomy during the second year of life lies in the maturation of the muscle system. Providing a safe environment for exploration is one of the best ways to help toddlers develop autonomy as well as healthy muscles. As they explore, they exercise their muscles and enhance muscle maturation by experimenting with such activities as holding on and letting go (and yes, dropping that spoon over and over is helping them develop their sense of autonomy and their brains). Children who are confined too much will not have the opportunity to develop a strong sense of autonomy. They need the opportunity to explore and test what they can and cannot do.

> Children who are confined too much will not have the opportunity to develop a strong sense of autonomy. They need the opportunity to explore and test what they can and cannot do.

Jenny did not know about the importance of helping her toddler develop a strong sense of autonomy. She was an artist who loved to paint during the day when the light was good. Her daughter, Dani, seemed content to sit in a high chair eating crackers for long periods of time. When Dani would tire of

the high chair, Jenny would move her to a playpen or windup swing.
Dani was rarely let out to roam around the house.

Jenny was not a "bad" parent. She felt thrilled and lucky that Dani seemed so content with her confinement and that she could get so much painting done. Jenny didn't understand that she was hindering Dani's development of autonomy and muscle development by not giving her more opportunities to explore. As we discussed in chapter 4, lack of physical and intellectual stimulation can also hamper optimal brain development.

Positive Discipline methods help children develop a sense of autonomy as well as the characteristics and the life skills they need when they can no longer depend on adults. Children, from birth through the preschool years, always need adults around. They also need opportunities to start developing the attitudes and skills they will need for the rest of their childhood and adult lives when parents are not around.

Punishment does not foster a healthy sense of autonomy and it does not teach life skills, but *not* punishing seems to require a real shift in attitude for many parents. Punishment (spanking and shaming children for doing things that are developmentally appropriate) fosters doubt and shame. Children will experience enough self-imposed doubt and shame as they encounter the real limits of their abilities. Hopefully, an understanding of this important developmental stage will help parents avoid adding to the frustration children experience as they progress in their desire for more independence.

Developmentally Appropriate Behavior

PATSY HAD HER *arms full. The diaper bag was slung over one shoulder, two overdue library books were gripped in one hand, and the car keys dangled precariously from one finger. Patsy's other arm cradled her two-month-old baby son.*

"Come on, Megan," she called to her two-and-a-half-year-old daughter (with just a bit of forced cheerfulness). "It's time to go to the library. Let's get in the car."

But Megan wasn't having anything to do with the idea. She stood miserably at the top of the porch steps with her arms stretched out toward her mother. "Up!" she insisted.

Patsy sighed with exasperation. "You can walk," she said encouragingly. "Come on, sweetie—Mommy's arms are full."

Megan's small face crumpled. "Can't walk," she wailed, collapsing in a pitiful little heap. "Uuuuppp!"

Patsy sighed and her overloaded shoulders sagged. Was it wrong to ask Megan to use her own two legs? Would she feel unloved if Patsy didn't pick her up?

It is developmentally appropriate to carry an infant but less appropriate to carry a toddler. This does not mean you never carry a two-year-old; it does mean you have an increased awareness of her need to develop autonomy.

Suppose you have a toddler who wants to be carried to the car. Instead of carrying her, you may stoop down, give her a hug (you may need to put a few things down first), and tell her you are sure she can walk to the car by herself. If she still whines to be carried, you might say, "I'll hold your hand and walk slowly, but I know you can do it." You might even add, "I really need your help. Will you carry my book?" (If it is a small one.) Yes, it would be easier to just pick her up and carry her to the car. Helping children develop the confidence and life skills they need is not always easy or convenient. But who said parenting would be easy? It need not be so difficult, either. Successful parenting is often a matter of knowing what is effective and what is not. (For more on developmentally appropriate behavior see chapter 9.)

Distraction and Choices

IT IS NORMAL and developmentally appropriate for toddlers to explore and want to touch, so it is wise to provide them with areas where they can do so safely.

In the kitchen, you might have a cupboard full of plastic containers, wooden spoons, pots and pans, and other items that can't hurt or be hurt by your child. In the living room, you can provide a box of special toys. When your child wants to touch something that shouldn't be touched, such as a stereo, kindly and firmly pick her up and remove her from that item and place her by the toy box. Don't slap or say "No!" Instead, say this: "You can play with your toys. Look at the big truck. I'll bet you can make it move." This is called distraction, and you may have to do it over and over and over. (Too many parents don't realize that they spank over and over, or say no over and over, or wrestle over the same table ornament daily. Adults can decide whether the expensive table ornament is in or out of little Jamie's reach. When we continue to repeat the same ineffective responses and then say that this child "never learns," we may need to wonder who the slow learner is. Distraction, much more peaceful for both parent and child, will be discussed in more detail in chapter 8.)

Children may experience frustration at not being allowed to play with the stereo or to run into the street. This is what Erikson called the real "crisis" of this stage of development. However, adding punishment to the natural crisis is like pouring salt on a wound. The frustration is greatly eased when parents remember to be kind when they are being firm. Children feel the difference. A word of caution: It still feels like punishment to the child if distraction is accompanied by shaming words, such as "bad girl."

Toddlers are interested in exploring so many things that it is not difficult to use distraction at this age. When a toddler wants to touch something that isn't appropriate, offer a substitute—or a choice of substitutes. "You can't jump on the couch. Would you like to play with your truck or help me wash the dishes?" "It is time for bed. Which story do you want me to read when you've put on your pajamas?" (Yes, toddlers can learn to put on their pajamas, with or without your help, depending on their age.) "I need to talk on the phone now. You can play in the junk drawer (prepared in advance with age-appropriate items) or the pan cupboard while I'm on the phone." One mom kept several activity baskets on top of her refrigerator. When she wanted to talk on the phone, she brought out a basket. Her daughter eagerly looked forward to a chance to play with her special toys. The baskets came down only during phone calls. With simple additions, such as a new koosh ball, a different-sized block, or a simple puzzle, the baskets remained intriguing. Offering choices and using distraction are simple and respectful responses to a toddler's need for guidance.

Don't Slap Hands or Spank

TO SPANK OR not to spank is another major parenting debate. In the context of autonomy versus doubt and shame, it is obvious that spanking fosters more doubt and shame than the child experiences from natural limits. (We will discuss discipline in greater detail in chapter 14.) A young child often does not understand the connection between what she did (reach for an electrical cord) and the response (a quick slap). Too many parents have had the unsettling experience of reaching for their child in love and having that child cringe away in fear, as if a slap is on the way—certainly not the sort of relationship that fosters trust and closeness and certainly not what most parents would choose.

> Offering choices and using distraction are simple and respectful responses to a toddler's need for guidance.

Use Training, Not Abandonment

SOME PARENTS MISTAKENLY believe that spanking is a good way to train children. Many parents say, "But I have to spank my children when it is a matter of life or death. I have to spank my child to teach her not to run into the street." But does spanking really teach your child what you intend? Even after you have spanked her, would you let her play near a busy street unsupervised?

Most parents are quick to realize that spanking is neither teaching nor training. Spanking and slapping are reactions often born out of fear, worry, and frustration. A parent might spank a child a hundred times, but even so, it would be unwise to allow that child to play unsupervised by a busy street. Children need to be supervised when they are near any kind of danger that requires mature judgment and skills. It is much more effective to teach children the judgment and skills to handle dangerous streets than it is to scare them by spanking. Your supervision, guidance, and warm, reassuring hand are essential.

How might you effectively deal with a child who has a fondness for the middle of the road? Take time for training every time you have the occasion to cross a busy street by asking your child to look both ways and tell you when no cars are coming. Ask your child to tell you when it is safe to cross the street. If you don't agree with his assessment, ask, "What about the big truck that's coming? What do you think will happen if that truck hits us?" Throughout this process, your child needs to be holding your hand. He is learning a skill. Sky divers do not get thrown out of the plane just because they recognize the pull cord on the parachute. Training and skill mastery are not synonymous. At least your child will not be learning that you are much scarier than the street!

How Do We Teach Toddlers?

TEACH BY ASKING questions, and encourage your toddler to ask questions, too. (The importance of asking "what" and "how" questions is discussed in more detail in chapter 7.) Skip the lectures. They invite avoidance or resistance, while questions invite thinking and participation. Education comes from the Latin root *educare,* which means "to draw forth." Questions draw forth. Lectures attempt to stuff in—a method that usually fails.

> Skip the lectures. They invite avoidance or resistance, while questions invite thinking and participation.

Toddlers can understand more than they can verbalize. Asking questions such as, "What might happen if we cross the street without looking first?" helps with their language development, their thinking skills, and their sense of autonomy.

I Blew It!

SOMETIMES PARENTS FEEL guilty when they discover new information, especially when it seems to point out mistakes they may have made. You may be saying, "Oh my goodness! That's what I did! Have I ruined my children forever?" Absolutely not! As we say over and over, mistakes are wonderful opportunities to learn—for adults and for children.

Sometimes we need to tell our children about our mistakes and start over. "Honey, I thought the best way to show you how much I love you was to do everything for you. Now I know that is not the best thing for you. It may be hard for both of us when I stop being a supermom and help you learn how capable you are, but I have faith in both of us. We can do it!" And it's true. Don't waste any time on guilt. You will continue to make mistakes; so will your children. Isn't that exciting? If your child isn't talking yet, you can convey the same message through the energy of your attitude and confidence.

Understanding the importance of this developmental age can help parents learn the skills and provide the atmosphere (at least, most of the time) that encourages children to learn important competency skills that will serve them all their lives. Parents can also interact with their children (most of the time) in ways that invite them to make healthy decisions about themselves, others, and the world. Notice we said "invite." We can never be sure how individuals will interpret their own life experiences and what they will decide about them. Notice, too, that we say "most of the time." None of us—parents or children—gets it right all the time. Teaching, loving, and acting respectfully most of the time really is enough.

Unconscious Life Decisions

ONE THING CHILDREN do not consciously understand and cannot verbalize is the unconscious decisions they are constantly making about themselves, about the world, about others, and about how they need to behave in the world to survive and thrive. They are making these decisions based on their interpretation of their life experiences.

When you distract her by removing her from what she can't touch and guide her to what she can touch, what will she decide? That it is okay to explore, to try new things, to learn about the world around her. Which lesson do you want to teach? Distraction does not damage her self-esteem or self-confidence like spanking and shaming can. It does let her know that some things are acceptable to touch and some are unacceptable. Self-esteem begins here. The seeds are planted early.

A child may still feel frustrated and upset about not being allowed to touch whatever she

> Distraction does not damage her self-esteem or self-confidence like spanking and shaming can. It does let her know that some things are acceptable to touch and some are unacceptable. Self-esteem begins here.

wants. She may even have a temper tantrum. However, when supervised with firmness and kindness, she will be left with a much different feeling than when she is controlled with force or punishment.

Children who are encouraged to develop a sense of autonomy will usually make healthier decisions later in life. Children who are not allowed to develop a sense of autonomy will more often make decisions based on doubt and shame.

Love and Enjoyment

IT ALWAYS COMES back to love and enjoyment. Nothing is more important to the emotional development of your child. Understanding how important it is for a child to develop autonomy can help parents know that overprotection is not the best way to show love. Instead, they can have fun showing love by watching freedom and independence develop in their children and by enjoying the promise of confidence and courage in years to come.

7

The Value of Autonomy

"Me Do It"

"ME DO IT!" These words are the cry of the eager two-year-old who is trying to tell us, "I'm ready for big-time autonomy." Do we listen? Or do we say, "No, you're too little. You can't do it well enough. Wait until you're bigger. It is easier and faster for me to do it." Parents often do not realize that by saying these familiar words, they may have halted the unfurling of a budding sense of autonomy. Years later, those same parents may find themselves wondering why their child "just won't do anything!"

Again, we are talking about a sense of autonomy—not actual ability. In the first year children develop a sense of trust or a sense of mistrust. The second year is the beginning of a sense of autonomy or a sense of doubt and shame, which intensifies in the third year.

Jeremy is almost three years old, and while his parents often laugh that he is a "handful," they delight in their son's curiosity and willingness to experiment with and experience the world around him. Jeremy's mother discovered him one bright morning making a cake in the kitchen; he had stirred milk, raisins, two eggs (with shells), Cheerios, and lots of flour in the largest bowl he could find. Jeremy's dad found him a few days later with a screwdriver and pliers, investigating the inner workings of the vacuum cleaner. Jeremy, his parents have decided, needs invitations to help in the kitchen, a set of his own small tools (and nonelectrical objects to experiment with)—and lots of supervision. Despite the occasional messes, they're happy to know that their son finds his world a fascinating and welcoming place.

Matthew is also nearly three years of age, but Matthew's world is a different sort of place than Jeremy's. Matthew is most comfortable in front of the television, watching a video. New people and places frighten him and he rarely speaks, although his parents often encourage him not to be "so shy." Matthew loves the computer and tried to help his dad with his work, but something happened to Dad's files and Dad got mad. Matthew would like to work in the garden with his mom, too, but after he dug a whole row of small holes for her to put plants in, she sighed the big sigh that Matthew hates and told him to go play in the house. It feels safer to Matthew not to have too many ideas, and when people raise their voices he hunches into a small ball. It will take some time and a lot of encouragement for Matthew to show his curiosity again.

Venturing Out: The Value of Autonomy

TWO-YEAR-OLDS see the world as an exciting and fascinating place, especially as they develop more autonomy and a greater physical and intellectual capacity to explore. At the same time, however, they are often frustrated when adults get in their way. They experience frustration when they find they do not have the skills or abilities to get some of the things they want or cannot accomplish what they want to. Children may respond to these frustrations by withdrawing and adopting a sense of doubt about their ability to "conquer the world." Adults can help develop toddlers' confidence by providing a range of opportunities, time for training, and encouragement for the many things children can do so they have the opportunity to gain a sense of autonomy that is stronger than their sense of doubt.

Intention: Is This Really Misbehavior?

PARENTING A TODDLER will be much less frustrating when parents respond to the intention behind the behavior. This is often more easily said than done, especially when you're face-to-face with a two-year-old in a temper. Still, page 76 has a few points to consider that may help you work with your child's development and needs.

AUTONOMY INTERCEPTED

Nature pushes in one direction and often adults tug in another. Frustration results. Adults have a name for this frustration: they call it "misbehavior." It is important to understand how discouragement (and misbehavior) might be related to a child's frustration regarding the development of autonomy. It takes a spunky child to keep fighting for his need to develop autonomy when parents and teachers are trying to control him. Is Johnnie's defiance thwarted autonomy? Has little Mary figured out how to manipulate others to get her way because of improper autonomy guidance? Has Timmy withdrawn into helplessness, insisting that you do everything for him, because he feels discouraged about his ability to do things for himself? Whenever your child misbehaves in these ways, you might ask yourself, "Could it be that this behavior is founded in discouragement because I have not used kindness and firmness to help my child develop a healthy sense of autonomy?"

- *"Defiance" looks (and feels) much different when we understand that a child is struggling to develop a sense of autonomy.* This means that her perception of a situation may be very different from yours. Does this mean that it's okay for your two-year-old to shout "No!" in your face? No—but it may mean that you should respond in a different way. (As we will undoubtedly say again, encounters usually go more smoothly when only one of you is having a tantrum.)

- *It makes sense that a child doesn't listen to you when you understand that his developmental urges have a "louder voice."* He doesn't intend to disobey or to forget what you've asked; your requests and instructions are simply overwhelmed by his own needs and developmental process.

- *It makes sense to use kindness and firmness instead of punishment or useless lectures ("How many times do I have to tell you?") when you understand developmental appropriateness.* The kindness shows love and respect for your child's needs and limitations; the firmness provides structure, teaching, and safety.

Adults also may need a slight attitude adjustment. We sometimes expect certain abilities and behavior from young children, then we are disappointed or angry when they don't live up to our expectations. Two-year-olds are too little to do things perfectly. Which is more important—perfection or helping your child develop healthy self-esteem and strong life skills? Of course it is simpler and faster for you to do things for your child instead of taking the time and having the patience to help him do things (such as dressing) himself. Which is more important—ease and speed or helping children develop confidence and an ability to learn from mistakes?

Who ever said parenting was easy? Quick and efficient? Tidy? Too many parents want confident, courageous, cooperative, respectful, resourceful, responsible children, but they don't understand what children need in order to develop these characteristics.

One purpose of this book is to give parents and caregivers the kind of discipline skills that help children develop trust and autonomy as well as crucial values and life skills. Since autonomy does not equal ability, and since skills take time to learn, training is essential for the child to develop a sense of autonomy.

With training, two-year-olds can dress themselves, pour their own cereal and milk, and help set the table. They can learn to help out at the grocery store, join in activities at church, or behave in other public places. Learning these kinds of skills is an important part of developing a sense of autonomy.

> Who ever said parenting was easy? Quick and efficient? Tidy? Too many parents want confident, courageous, cooperative, respectful, resourceful, responsible children, but they don't understand what children need in order to develop these characteristics.

Skills Are Learned, Not Inborn

NO ONE IS born with an ability to eat with a spoon. There are no genetic codes connected to being able to ease one's arms into narrow coat sleeves. Even child prodigies cannot carry a full cup of juice without losing a drop or two. Skills are learned—not inborn. When we understand that all skills require training, we see children as competent learners with unlimited potential. Otherwise, we are tempted to regard them as inept miniatures, helpless at best, clumsy and burdensome at worst.

One of the most exciting insights of brain research tells us that brain connections strengthen with repetition. This applies directly to skill development. Young Elizabeth might not perfect the art of fitting her feet into her shoes on the first try. It requires regular

> When we understand that all skills require training, we see children as competent learners with unlimited potential.

repetition of this act to achieve proficiency. Her brain is truly mastering the skill by linking up new connections while she works persistently with her chubby fingers and squirmy toes, holding her tongue precariously between her new mouthful of teeth. Research has taught us that knowledge and experience are inseparably entwined; each increases the other. When we teach children to master tasks step-by-step and provide lots of opportunities to practice, we create competent, confident children.

Skills Versus Spills

LIFE WITH TWO-YEAR-OLDS gets messy. The process of learning skills means there are lots of opportunities to spill, drip, and dump. Think of a typical activity: pouring morning cereal and milk. Part of training involves modifying the task to help little ones experience success.

The cereal box is big and unwieldy; so is the milk container. But we can adjust both so that children can practice autonomy and learn new skills. Serve milk in a little pitcher or measuring cup, repackage cereal in small plastic containers (margarine containers work well), and place everything at a convenient height. Demonstrate pouring the cereal, then add the milk. At first, let your child hold her hands on yours (to get a feel for the task), then rest yours lightly on top of hers as she repeats the movements. Finally, stay nearby and encourage her efforts.

What if there are spills? Part of learning to pour is spilling. Anticipate the need for another skill: wiping up puddles. Teach your child how to use a sponge, or provide a special floor rag or hang a mop nearby, one with a cutoff handle to make it child-sized. Celebrate as your child gradually masters these new skills.

Going Out in Public

WITH TIME FOR training, children can learn to behave in those famous child development observation laboratories: public places. Taking time for training can involve many strategies. Planning ahead, offering limited choices, and following through, as well as other techniques that will be discussed in greater detail in this chapter, can be used to help a child learn to behave when you're out in public.

Plan Ahead—or Expect Resistance Ahead

Young children live in the present moment. The world consists of things directly in front of them. When we shift their world by placing them in a different setting, even one they experience regularly, they may resist. A shift from playing with blocks in the living room to rolling along in a grocery basket takes considerable adjustment, and some children find it easier than others do (more about this

THE FIVE BEST WAYS TO PROVIDE SKILL TRAINING FOR YOUR CHILDREN

1. Plan ahead—or expect resistance ahead.

2. Involve children in the planning process.

3. Offer limited choices.

4. Ask "what" and "how" questions.

5. Follow through with dignity and respect.

when we discuss temperament in chapter 8). A resisting two-year-old does not show off skills to advantage—his or ours.

When moving from one activity or location to another, planning ahead is critical. Your young explorer will want to climb under the clothing racks, sneak a peek at the world from the top of the chair, and mount an expedition to discover what lies beyond the corner—any corner. Planning ahead is like painting a picture. If you skip details, the final picture may be blurry.

Involve Children in the Planning Process

You might set the stage something like this: "We are going to eat with Aunt Annie and Cousin Jamie at the restaurant. Before we get there, what will you do in the car?" (If a child is preverbal, use simple language to describe the event. If she is verbal, allow her to supply the answers as the planning proceeds.) Mention the car seat, buckling in, and playing with toys en route. You can explore the coming occasion with your child using simple questions and descriptions.

Invite your child to picture the setting or describe it for her: sitting in the chair, drawing with special crayons, and eating up all her lunch. What will she be allowed to order? Must she eat things she doesn't like? Bit by bit, the picture grows. Be sure to clarify expectations—and keep them realistic.

"When you finish eating, should you throw your food? What about running around the restaurant? Is it okay to grab the sugar container?" Do not get carried away with don'ts. Focus more on a clear picture of do's. Remember, "let's pretend" is often a painless, enjoyable way to establish limits and expectations.

Be sure the plans include your child's needs as well as those of the social situation. How long can she sit still during a meal? What activities are available? How does time to play with her cousins fit into the picture? Perhaps this outing would be better held at a fast-food restaurant than at an elegant candlelit brunch. Remember: plan for success—everyone's! Train in simple settings before expecting Olympic-level performance.

Offer Limited Choices

A great way to encourage autonomy involves offering choices. The choices must be appropriate and clearly defined, and they must be choices with which the adult can live. For example, the following choices might cause problems:

- "Would you like to go to child care today?" (This is the adult's responsibility and often isn't a choice but a necessity.)

- "What would you like to do today?" (The child needs some hints here. Are we talking coloring, baking cookies, or a trip to Disneyland?)

- "You may pick out any toy you want; you get to choose." (Does this include the $200 motorized kiddie-car *and* the Little Golden book? Be sure you can keep the promises you make. It is usually wise to think carefully before speaking!)

> Be sure you can keep the promises you make. It is usually wise to think carefully before speaking!

Myrna and Lamar Johnson decided they would teach their son Mark to dress himself when he was two years old (excellent training for budding initiative). They purchased clothes that were easy for a small child to manage, such as pants with elastic bands, wide-neck T-shirts, and sneakers with Velcro fasteners. Mark was a willing student and pretty much mastered the art of dressing himself (even though he put his shoes on the wrong feet about half of the time). He got to select his outfits, and both Myrna and Lamar learned to remain silent, even if Mark's color scheme left something to be desired. Myrna and Lamar were thoughtful about which choices they offered Mark. These did not include swimsuits in winter, rain boots in mid-July, or complicated overalls that he could not possibly fasten himself. Inherent in these choices was a successful outcome.

Ask "What" and "How" Questions

Children do not develop a strong sense of autonomy when parents and teachers spend too much time lecturing—telling children what happened, what caused it to happen, how they should feel about it, and what they should do about it. Telling may keep children from seeing mistakes as opportunities to learn. Telling instills doubt because it sends the message that children aren't living up to adult expectations. Lecturing often goes over children's heads because they're not ready to understand the concepts adults are trying to establish—and they usually discover they can simply tune adults out (unintentional training in the art of not listening). Last but not least, telling children what, how, and why teaches them what to think, not *how* to think. Parents are often disappointed when their children don't develop more self-control without realizing they are not using the kind of parenting skills that encourage self-control.

A powerful way to help children develop thinking skills, judgment skills, problem-solving skills, and autonomy is to ask them, "What happened? What were you trying to do? Why do you think this happened? How do you feel about it? How could you fix it? What else could you do if you don't want this to happen again?"

Remember that the world is a brand-new place for young children. At one preschool, a two-year-old pulled his gloves off to scoop up handfuls of snow. After a minute or two, he came to his teacher in tears. His hands hurt! He had

> A powerful way to help children develop thinking skills, judgment skills, problem-solving skills, and autonomy is to ask them, "What happened? What were you trying to do? Why do you think this happened? How do you feel about it? How could you fix it? What else could you do if you don't want this to happen again?"

no idea that his hands were terribly cold, nor that the sensation had anything to do with the exciting white stuff covering the playground. Snow was rare in this child's town and he had never seen it before. The teacher warmed his hands, replaced his mittens, and showed him how much better his hands felt when they weren't touching the snow directly. He gained new information, added another life experience to his small portion, and was careful to keep his mittens in place the rest of the morning.

When children are younger, they need more clues as part of the "what" and "how" questions. For example, if a two-year-old gets stuck on her tricycle, she will be invited to think and use initiative if you ask, "What do you think would happen if you got off and backed up?" This is very different from telling her to get off and back up. Even though a question contains direct clues, it still invites thought and a decision. As children get older, they will benefit from questions with fewer clues.

Follow Through with Dignity and Respect

Again, we want to stress that permissiveness is not the way to help children develop autonomy. One alternative to permissiveness is kind and firm follow-through.

What might follow-through look like in the restaurant meal described earlier? Mom might have explained in advance that if her daughter had trouble remembering how to behave in the restaurant, they would have to leave. Kind and firm follow-through means that if she misbehaves, Mom will take her out to wait in the car together while the others in the group finish their meal. It is not respectful to scold or spank while removing her. Respect requires kindness and firmness at the same time. A parent can either say nothing or say firmly (but kindly), "I'm sorry you didn't feel like behaving in the restaurant today. You can try again later or perhaps next time."

Giving a child a chance to try again next time is reasonable and encouraging. It is not reasonable to say, "I'm never taking you out to eat again—or anywhere else, for that matter!" Besides being unreasonable, most parents do not follow through on such threats. This does not demonstrate kindness or firmness, nor does it inspire trust.

Yes, it is inconvenient for you to miss your meal at the restaurant while using kind and firm follow-through. You also have a choice. Which is more important, a restaurant meal or the self-esteem and confidence your child will develop by learning appropriate social skills? When you follow through with kindness and firmness, you won't have to miss many meals before your child learns that you say what you mean—and that you will do what you say. When we follow through, we also teach our children another important form of trust: parents are reliable and can be counted on to act on their words—without making the child feel blame and shame ("I may not like it that I didn't get my way, but at least my parents don't heap blame and shame on to my frustration").

> Giving a child a chance to try again next time is reasonable and encouraging. It is not reasonable to say, "I'm never taking you out to eat again—or anywhere else, for that matter!" Besides being unreasonable, most parents do not follow through on such threats. This does not demonstrate kindness or firmness, nor does it inspire trust.

Out of Control

Q. *My two-and-a-half-year-old son is out of control! He doesn't know what the words "Wait, please!" mean. (Well, he knows—but he doesn't want to hear about it.) If he doesn't get you to jump at his every command, he throws a fit or goes on like a broken record repeating over and over again what he wants. When out in public lately he has been really out of control. He will kick and hit me and scream at the top of his lungs to get what he wants. Last time it was*

*because I told him we had to leave the jungle gym at the park. He didn't
want to leave and made such a scene that everyone was watching. What
do I do in this situation? I don't believe in hitting him, yet I don't appreciate being hit and humiliated like this, either. I am at the end of my rope
with him. Some days I feel like I could snap and lose it with him, the way
he has been acting. I feel like I have no control at all with him. He never
ever listens to me. Any advice would be appreciated.*

A. Some people would call your toddler "spirited"; others might
label him "strong-willed." Whatever you call him, trying to *control*
him will never work.

However, there are three ways you can increase cooperation:

1. Your child does not understand "Wait, please!" in the way you
think he does. This is an abstract concept that is in direct opposition
to his developmental need to explore his world and his growing
sense of autonomy. This is the "me do it" stage. This does not mean
he should be allowed to do anything he wants. It does mean that all
methods to gain cooperation should be kind and firm at the same
time instead of controlling and/or punitive.

2. Instead of telling him what to do, find ways to involve him in
the decision so he gets a sense of personal power and autonomy. For
example:

- *Give him some warning.* "We need to leave in a minute. What
  is the last thing you want to do on the jungle gym?"

- *Carry a small timer around with you.* Let him help you set it
  to one or two minutes. Then let him put the timer in his
  pocket so he can be ready to go when the timer goes off.

- *Give him a choice that requires his help.* "Do you want to carry
  my purse to the car, or do you want to carry the keys?" Help
  him visualize the next activity. "What is the first thing we
  should do when we get home?"

3. If these don't work, you may need to take him by the hand and lead him to the car. Every time he resists, stop pulling and let your hand go in his direction until he stops resisting. Then pull toward the car again, giving slack every time he resists. This may look like a seesaw. When he catches on that you are going to be *both kind and firm,* he will eventually go with you. If not, you may need to pick him up and carry him to the car while ignoring his kicks and screams. The key is to avoid the "emotional hook" (that feeling we get as parents that we have to "win" or enforce our will) that invites a power struggle every time.

Living with—and Learning from—Mistakes

BY NOW YOU might be afraid that you have to be a perfect parent to raise a healthy child. There is no such thing. Isn't that wonderful? Parents and children are alike in one important respect: they never stop making mistakes. It doesn't matter how much we learn or how much we know. As human beings, we sometimes forget what we know and get hooked into emotional reactions. Sometimes we just goof up. Once we accept this, we can see mistakes as the important life processes they are: interesting opportunities to learn.

Wouldn't it be wonderful if we could instill this attitude in our children so they wouldn't be burdened with all the baggage we carry about mistakes? Many children (and adults) short-circuit the lifelong process of developing a healthy sense of autonomy (and fail to develop the courage it requires to take risks and try new things) because they are afraid to make mistakes. Mistakes aren't the same as failures, although we often behave as though they are. Asking "what" and "how" questions will help tremendously as we work our way through the learning process.

"Oh, Joy!" or "Oh, Boy!"

THERE IS SO much to learn. The toddler years are messy, inconvenient, and certainly time-consuming. These little folks only get to see the world through brand-new eyes once. Our job is to share with them in that spirit of adventure—even when we do it from the backseat of a car while everyone else enjoys dinner inside the restaurant. With a change of perspective (and an occasional deep breath or two), we can see the joy of these months—at least most of the time.

We'll say it again: love and joy. The more we learn about what is developmentally appropriate and how we can enhance the environment in which children grow, the more we learn the skills that will encourage them to reach their full potential (as well as forgive ourselves when we make mistakes), and the more we can relax and just enjoy watching our children grow—knowing that they're learning to trust their own abilities, believe in the suport of the adults in their lives, and experience the wonder of life all around them.

PART THREE

Getting to Know
Your Unique Child

Temperament and
Age Appropriateness

There is an old saying that each person is like all other people, like some other people, and like no other person. Until we share our life with a young child, however, most of us fail to realize just how true that saying is.

All young children share similar traits and developmental stages. However, children are never exactly alike, even when they're "identical" twins. Therein lies one of the great mysteries—and challenges—of parenting. Who is this little person, anyway? And why does she do the things she does?

In the next two chapters we will discover ways of learning to know your unique child. We will explore temperament and the effect it has on how your child responds to her world. We will also take a look at how your child's age and special qualities affect her behavior—and how you can guide and shape it.

8

Temperament

What Makes Your
Child Unique?

MOST PARENTS AND teachers cherish a fantasy about having "the perfect baby" or "the perfect child." The conventional description of this ideal baby is one who doesn't cry or fuss very often, who sleeps peacefully through the night, takes long naps, eats her food without spitting it out (or up), and who can happily entertain herself, gurgling and cooing angelically at her crib mobile. "Oh," we say when confronted with one of these enviable specimens, "what a good baby." Does this mean that all babies who don't fit this description are "bad"?

The Myth of the Perfect Child

OF COURSE, THERE is no such thing as a "bad" baby or child, even though most don't fit the fantasy description. Babies are born with different, unique personalities, as any parent with more than one child knows.

Frankly, we worry about a child who fits the fantasy description. Usually this is a child who doesn't feel secure enough to test power boundaries and find out who she is apart from her parents and teachers, who is afraid to make mistakes or risk disapproval. We say "usually" because a few babies do fit the fantasy description and still feel secure and aren't afraid to make mistakes. They are called "easy" children.

> Babies are born with different, unique personalities, as any parent with more than one child knows.

Drs. Stella Chess and Alexander Thomas investigated the miracle of personality in their longitudinal study of the nine major temperaments found in children. These temperaments—the qualities and characteristics that contribute to individual personalities—serve to describe three types of children: the "easy" child, the "difficult" child, and the "slow to warm up" child. All are good; some are just more challenging than others! We will discuss these nine temperaments, but for more information we highly recommend *Know Your Child* by Stella Chess and Alexander Thomas.

Recent research on how the human brain grows is adding to our understanding of temperament and personality. How babies and toddlers interact with their parents and other caregivers appears to have a strong effect on how their inborn tendencies actually develop. It's a complex process, one that we don't yet fully understand. But it seems clear that the relationship between an infant and the important adults in his or her life can shape the development of that child's temperament—knowledge that gives us both a wonderful opportunity and a serious responsibility.

The Berkeley Studies

SCIENTIFIC INVESTIGATION OF temperament theory began in the late sixties and seventies with the Berkeley Studies, a longitudinal study of two basic temperaments, active and passive. This study revealed that these two temperaments were lifelong characteristics; in other words, passive infants grew up to be passive adults, while active infants grew up to be active adults. Actually, activity levels can be measured in the womb.

Chess and Thomas expanded the temperament theory significantly, even though their nine temperaments all fit under the general headings of active and passive. A major benefit of being aware of temperament differences is that parents and caregivers can better understand their children, learn to respond to them in ways that encourage development and growth, and learn to appreciate and accept them as they are. With understanding and acceptance, parents and teachers are equipped to help children reach their full potential rather than trying to mold them into perfect fantasy children.

The Nine Temperaments

THE NINE TEMPERAMENTS ARE: activity level, rhythmicity, initial response (approach or withdrawal), adaptability, sensory threshold, quality of mood, intensity of reactions, distractibility, and persistence and attention span. All children possess varying degrees of each characteristic. The following sections will describe what they look like in real life (you may want to think about children you know as we examine these aspects of temperament).

Activity Level

Activity level refers to the level of motor activity and the proportion of active and inactive periods. For instance, an infant with high activity might kick and splash so much in his bath that the floor needs a good mopping afterward, while a low-activity infant can turn over but doesn't often choose to do so. Activity level will influence a parent's interactions with a child. The parents of high-activity infants dash about like perpetual motion machines, trying to keep up with their busy infants.

Barry's mom lay next to her six-month-old on a beach blanket, pleading for his cooperation. "Could you just stay still for a few minutes?" she asked, as more sand from a vigorously kicking foot sprayed her face.

Two years later, Barry's mom found herself tiptoeing into the nursery at regular intervals. She would place her finger next to Baby Jeremy's nose to reassure herself that he was still breathing. After raising Barry, she could not quite believe that a baby might sleep for such long stretches of time.

Rhythmicity

Rhythmicity refers to the predictability (or unpredictability) of biological functions, such as hunger, sleeping, and bowel movements. One infant might have one bowel movement daily, immediately after breakfast, while another infant's schedule seems different each day. One child might eat her biggest meal at lunch, while another child prefers dinner—or a different meal each day!

Carla Jackson was so proud: she thought her little Jackie was toilet trained by the time he was two years old. She put him on his toilet chair several times a day, and he obligingly produced a bowel movement each morning and urinated on each succeeding visit. But Jackie wasn't toilet trained—his mom was trained. Jackie was so regular that when his mom remembered to put him on his chair, he performed. Whenever they were in a different setting and Carla forgot to put him on his chair, Jackie would have an "accident." Jackie stopped having accidents when he was three—and really toilet trained.

Carla's other children were not so regular, and she reproached herself for having "failed" to train them. Learning about temperament helped her to realize that she hadn't succeeded or failed; her children simply had different temperaments of regularity, as well as other differences.

Approach or Withdrawal

This temperament describes the way a child reacts to a new situation or stimulus, such as a new food, toy, person, or place. Approach responses are often displayed by mood expression (smiling, speech, facial expression) or motor activity (swallowing a new food, reaching for a new toy). Withdrawal responses look more negative and are expressed by mood (crying, fussing, speech, facial expression) or motor activity (moving away, spitting food out, pushing a new toy away). Learning to parent your unique child means recognizing these cues and responding in encouraging, nurturing ways.

Some babies are open to just about any new experience—new foods, new people—while others are more reluctant. One family experienced a special problem:

> *Ted Vasquez traveled several weeks each month as part of his job. When he returned home and attempted to pick up Isabelle, his new daughter, she would stiffen, resist, and begin crying. Ted felt devastated. He adored his baby girl. When he learned about temperament, he began to understand that his daughter simply reacted to changes of any kind with initial alarm. He began to take a gentler, more gradual approach after his prolonged absences. While his wife held Isabelle, he tickled the baby's feet, stroked her arms, and talked softly to her. Though Isabelle still was slow to warm up, this method allowed her more time to adjust. In the meantime, Ted no longer felt rejected but could be sympathetic to his daughter's needs.*

Some babies are open to just about any new experience— new foods, new people —while others are more reluctant.

Adaptability

Adaptability describes how a child reacts to a new situation over time—her ability to adjust and change. Some children initially spit out a new food but accept it after a few trial tastes. Others accept a new food, a new article of clothing, or a new preschool far more slowly, if at all.

Mary Wong was sure her nine-month-old had somehow learned to separate his infant cereal from the mashed bananas, carefully ejecting only the offensive cereal. Getting him to try new foods was a constant challenge. Mary learned to add only the tiniest taste and increase the amount gradually throughout the following days, until he was able to accept the new addition without complaint.

When Jenna Frank's baby arrived, the baby's older sister and brother were already in grade school and involved in a whirl of sports, music lessons, and other activities. Because of their busy schedule, the baby was rarely at home for a regular nap time. But that posed no problem: this baby was a highly adaptable child, perfectly content to curl up and sleep wherever he happened to be at the time, whether at a basketball game or in the grocery cart.

A key to understanding your child is to understand her temperament. What degree does your child have of each of the following temperament categories?

1. Activity level

2. Rhythmicity

3. Initial response (approach or withdrawal)

4. Adaptability

5. Sensory threshold

6. Quality of mood

7. Intensity of reactions

8. Distractibility

9. Persistence and attention span

Kate Knapp already had a son when her daughter was born, but she often found herself looking for rides for her son when activities occurred during the baby's nap time. If they weren't home at the proper time, the baby fell apart, crying, whining, and fussing. She wouldn't fall asleep anywhere except in her own bed. She would stay awake well past midnight if her family happened to be away from home. This baby had low adaptability, and all the family members suffered when they didn't take her temperament into account.

Sensory Threshold

Some children wake up from a nap every time a door opens, no matter how softly, while others can sleep through a hurricane. The level of sensitivity to sensory input varies from one child to the next and affects how they behave and view the world.

When Marjorie was eight months old, her grandmother took her outside to play. The day was warm and the yard sported a soft, new lawn. The moment Marjorie's knees touched the grass, her bottom popped into the air. She balanced herself with her hands and feet clutching the ground, avoiding contact between her bare knees and the tickly grass.

The same afternoon, Marjorie's cousin, Nellie, arrived for a visit. Nellie's mother plopped her down on the grass, and Nellie crawled off, not even slowing down when she crossed a gravel pathway. Nellie's high sensory threshold allowed her to be an intrepid explorer, while Marjorie's approach turned tentative in response to new textures and experiences.

Quality of Mood

Have you ever noticed how some children (and adults) react to life with pleasure and acceptance while others can find fault with everything and everybody? One baby might favor her family with smiles and coos, while another feels compelled to cry a bit, just "because."

Parents of less sunny little ones can take heart. Those tiny scowls are not in response to you or your parenting skills. Be sensitive to his mood, but take time to stroke your sober little fellow, massage his chubby cheeks, and share your own sunshine with him. As he grows, help him to see the world for the lovely place it is.

If your baby beams a happy face to the world, enjoy the gift her temperament brings to your life. Don't rain on her parade. Take a moment to savor the day through her rosy outlook.

Intensity of Reactions

Children often respond to events around them in different ways. Some smile quietly or merely take a look, then go back to what they were doing; others react with action and emotion.

The howls of your high-intensity baby can be heard throughout the apartment complex when she wakes up, while your neighbor's son just gives a little whimper.

At play group, Maya had her hair pulled by an inquisitive class-mate. The teacher panicked, sure from the way Maya hollered that she required a trip to the emergency room. When the same miscreant pulled Juan's hair, Juan hardly looked up from his blocks, swatting the other child's hand away as though it were no more than a fly alighting nearby.

Maya's mom has learned to sit quietly, waiting until Maya's initial reaction subsides to evaluate the seriousness of the situation. Juan's mother becomes truly alarmed when he cries loudly, knowing how much it takes to elicit such a response. Both children and parents have learned to interact differently based on the intensity of each child's reactions.

Distractibility

"If I sit my toddler down with a box of blocks, he won't notice anything else in the room," says one father. "Well," shares a mother, "if someone walks by while my baby is nursing, she not only looks but stops sucking until the person is gone." Another mom adds, "I've noticed that my daughter simply can't concentrate on eating when the whole family is at the table. I have to feed her ahead of the rest of us." They may not realize it, but these parents are actually talking about their children's distractibility, the way in which an outside stimulus interferes with a child's present behavior and his willingness (or unwillingness) to be diverted.

Joe heads for the stereo every time he comes into the living room. His sitter picks him up, carries him to his toy box, and sometimes even succeeds in distracting him for a moment or two. But minutes later, he sets his course for the stereo with an accuracy any pilot would admire. Joe might have a future as a pilot, able to stay on course, single-minded and focused. For now, his weary sitter must make yet another trip to remove his wiggling fingers from the delicate stereo knobs.

Ben picks up his dad's beeper, bringing it to his open mouth for a taste. Dad intercepts, tickling Ben and substituting a piece of toast. Ben gurgles, hardly noticing that the object clutched in his hand has changed. Ben's distractibility makes him an easy child to watch, while Joe's sitter is working up the courage to ask for an increase in pay.

Persistence and Attention Span

Persistence refers to a child's willingness to pursue an activity in the face of obstacles or difficulties; attention span describes the length of time he will pursue an activity without interruption. The two characteristics are usually related. A toddler who is content to tear up an old magazine for half an hour at a time has a fairly long attention span, while another who plays with ten different toys in ten minutes has a short one. Again, no combination is necessarily better than another; they're simply different and present different challenges in parenting and teaching.

Little Jennifer has experienced quite a growth spurt. Her added inch in height now prevents her from walking under the table, a feat she formerly did with ease, without stooping. Unfortunately, Jennifer has not yet figured this out. She spent the morning walking into the table, bumping her head each time. She yelled and raged at the table, determined to walk under it as she had so many times before. It is a toss-up which is more persistent, the table or Jennifer.

Baby Edith has spent the past half-hour sitting in her high chair, lining up rows of Cheerios. Sometimes she finds one big enough to fit onto her finger. Her twin sister, Emma, did not even make it through breakfast before her cereal, bowl, and cup hit the floor. Emma dismantled the pot and pan cupboard, explored the heating vent, and had to be retrieved from a foray into the bathroom—all while Edith patiently arranged her Cheerios. Edith might have a future as an accountant, while Emma might make a brilliant sportscaster. Edith's attention span extends for long periods, while Emma rarely stays with one thing for more than a few minutes—a talent that may someday help her keep up with rapidly changing game configurations and split-second moves. It is important to understand that both girls' temperaments can be strengths in the right situation. Wise parents and caregivers will help Emma and Edith maximize the potential of their inborn temperaments by providing teaching, nurturing—and lots of supervision.

Temperament: Challenge or Opportunity?

IF ASKED, MOST parents and teachers would probably prefer children with a long attention span and high persistence; they're much easier to teach and entertain. However, few children fit this ideal description. In fact, most families include children of different temperaments.

Parents and children have much to learn about each other during the first, critical months and years of life. Eventually, though, attentive and responsive parents learn to read the cues their children give them. One parent schedules activities with an eye to getting her baby home by nap time. He is very regular, slow to adapt, and becomes intensely distressed when his schedule is varied. Another family never needs to take nap time into account. Their adaptable and sunny-tempered child will just curl up and fall asleep whenever she gets tired, regardless of where she is.

Goodness of Fit

CHESS AND THOMAS emphasize the importance of "goodness of fit," the depth of understanding parents and teachers have of a child's temperament and their willingness to work with that child to encourage healthy development. Children experience enough stress in life as they struggle for competency and belonging. It does not help to compound that stress by expecting a child to be someone he is not.

Understanding a child's temperament doesn't mean shrugging your shoulders and saying, "Oh well, that's just the way this child is." It is an invitation to help a child develop acceptable behavior and skills. For instance, a child with a short attention span will still need to learn to accept some structure. Offering limited choices is one way to be respectful of the child's needs and of the "needs of the situation" (behavior appropriate for the present environment).

Working out a match between parents and children that meets the needs of both is critical to goodness of fit. If your child has an irregular sleep pattern and you can hardly keep your eyes open after being up night after night with your little owl, you have a poor fit. The key is to find the balance. Your baby might not sleep through the night due to her temperament, but she can learn to entertain

If asked, most parents and teachers would probably prefer children with a long attention span and high persistence; they're much easier to teach and entertain. However, few children fit this ideal description. In fact, most families include children of different temperaments.

herself when she wakes up. You may need to learn to stagger over and offer a gentle stroke or pat on the back, whisper a few loving words, then allow her to get back to sleep on her own. The first step is to determine what will work for all family members, with no one's needs being ignored. It is not in a child's best interest to have an exhausted, crabby parent. Yelling at, threatening, or totally ignoring a wakeful child also is not helpful. Finding the balance between your needs and those of your child can take some time and practice, but learning to accept and work with the individual, special temperament of your child will benefit you both as the years go by.

Many of the skills we suggest are appropriate for children of all temperaments, because they invite children to learn cooperation, responsibility, and life skills. However, an understanding of temperament helps us understand why different methods may be more effective, depending on the temperament and needs of an individual child.

Positive Discipline Skills for Parents and Caregivers

MANY OF THE skills we suggest are appropriate for children of all temperaments, because they invite children to learn cooperation, responsibility, and life skills. However, an understanding of temperament helps us understand why different methods may be more effective, depending on the temperament and needs of an individual child.

A child with a low sensory threshold may need a few moments alone to cry and release the tensions built up during a busy afternoon before settling down to fall asleep. It is respectful to provide this child with a quiet environment. It would not be appropriate to continue cooing to, cuddling, and generally overstimulating this little one. His sister, with her different sensory threshold, may thrive on lullabies, tickling games, and noisy family members careening through the halls.

A child with low distractibility will need patient preparation to switch from one activity to another. Planning ahead becomes a vital tool to smooth the way for transitions. A low-regularity parent living with a high-regularity toddler must learn to plan meals at predictable intervals, develop routines for daily activities, and establish a more defined rhythm to her day. Her child must learn to cope with occasional revised plans, survive on a cracker or two when a meal is delayed, and develop personal flexibility. The good news is that parents and children *can* adapt to each other. Our brains are programmed to respond to the world around us, and patience, sensitivity, and love can help all of us learn to live peacefully together.

Individuality and Creativity

PARENTS AND CAREGIVERS may not be aware of how they squelch individuality and creativity when they (often subconsciously) buy in to the myth of the perfect child. It is tempting for adults to prefer the "easy" child, or to want children to conform to the norms of society. Egos often get involved; we worry about what others think and fear that our competency may be questioned if our children aren't "good" in the eyes of others.

One of the primary motivators for the studies of Chess and Thomas was their desire to stop society's tendency to blame mothers for the characteristics of their children. Chess and Thomas state, "A child's temperament can actively influence the attitudes and behavior of her parents, other family members, playmates, and teachers, and in turn help to shape their effect on her behavioral development." In this way, the relationship between child and parents is a two-way street, each continuously influencing the other.

> Parents and caregivers may not be aware of how they squelch individuality and creativity when they (often subconsciously) buy in to the myth of the perfect child.

What if the mother whose twins behaved so differently had been two different mothers? It would have been easy to decide that quiet, focused Edith's mother was very effective, while active, busy Emma's mother "just couldn't control that child!" It may be wise to ask yourself occasionally, "Are you looking for blame, or are you looking for solutions?" The more we know about temperament and effective parenting skills, the better we will be at finding solutions that help our children develop into capable individuals, despite their differences and uniqueness.

Work for Improvement, Not Perfection

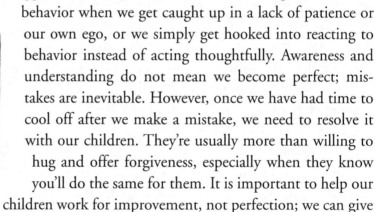

EVEN WITH UNDERSTANDING and the best intentions, most of us will struggle occasionally with our children's temperaments and behavior when we get caught up in a lack of patience or our own ego, or we simply get hooked into reacting to behavior instead of acting thoughtfully. Awareness and understanding do not mean we become perfect; mistakes are inevitable. However, once we have had time to cool off after we make a mistake, we need to resolve it with our children. They're usually more than willing to hug and offer forgiveness, especially when they know you'll do the same for them. It is important to help our children work for improvement, not perfection; we can give this gift to ourselves as parents and caregivers as well.

Kindness and Firmness

RUDOLF DREIKURS CONTINUALLY made a plea for parents and caregivers to use kindness and firmness with children. An understanding of temperament shows just how important this is. Kindness shows respect for the child and his uniqueness; firmness shows respect for the needs of the situation. By understanding and respecting your child's temperament, you will be able to help him reach his full potential as a capable, confident, contented person. And there's a bonus: you will probably get a lot more rest, laugh more, and learn a great deal about yourself and your child in the process.

9

Understanding Developmental and Age Appropriateness

AN UNDERSTANDING OF what is—and what is not—developmentally appropriate is one of the most useful parenting tools there is. As we discussed in chapter 5, it is developmentally appropriate to carry a baby in your arms. Being held, loved, and cuddled is helping him learn to trust. However, if your child seems to be too big to carry, he probably is. Many parents don't realize they are being disrespectful and discouraging when they give in to demands to carry a child who is capable of walking.

It is developmentally appropriate to discover and meet the needs of a crying infant by doing anything you can, but a crying toddler (or older child) will develop strong skills only if you help her learn to help herself instead of doing too much for her. Casey and his mom, Glenda, demonstrate how this might look:

Glenda gives Casey a glass of milk with his lunch. He looks at the glass and scowls. "Don't want this glass," he announces.

Glenda sighs in exasperation; then she recognizes an opportunity to teach her small son. "If you want another glass," she says gently, "what do you need to do to get it?"

Casey isn't particularly interested in learning at the moment. "Can't reach it," he whines.

Glenda asks, "What would happen if you pushed the chair over to the cupboard? Then what could you do?"

This new prospect captures Casey's imagination. He stops whining and thinks about it. "I could climb on the chair and reach the glass."

Glenda offers a choice. "Do you need my help pushing the chair over to the cupboard, or can you do it by yourself?"

With total enthusiasm, Casey says, "I can do it!"

He pushes the chair over to the cupboard, gets the glass, climbs down, and takes the glass over to the table, looking very proud of himself. Casey pours it from the old glass into the new one, creating several puddles of milk in the process.

Instead of becoming annoyed, Glenda recognizes more opportunities to teach. "What do you need to do now to clean up the milk you spilled?"

By now, Casey is feeling very capable. He jumps from the table, gets a sponge from under the sink, and cleans up the spilled milk. He leaves the sponge on the table.

Glenda continues, "Do you know what happens to milk when it is left in a sponge?"

Casey looks closely at the sponge but doesn't see anything happening. He is curious. "What?"

Glenda explains, "It turns sour and smells very bad. You'll need to rinse out the sponge in the sink really well before you put it back under the sink."

Casey never turns down an opportunity to play with water. He happily moves the chair over to the sink, climbs up, and rinses out the sponge. His mother teaches him how to squeeze it thoroughly to get all the milk out.

After the sponge is rinsed, Casey moves the chair back to the table and proudly sits down to drink his milk out of his special glass.

Time-consuming? Yes! Is it worth it? Yes! Casey has learned that his needs and desires are valid and that he is capable of taking care of them himself. It takes more than kind words to build self-esteem; it takes "competency experiences," moments when we and our children accept a challenge—and succeed. Casey's mother took the time to teach him the skills he needed to feel capable rather than encouraging manipulation intended to get other people to serve him. This is kind and firm, developmentally appropriate discipline in action.

Maintaining Dignity and Respect

WE REPEAT: we are not advocating permissiveness. Permissiveness is not healthy for children and does not teach them the life skills they need to learn. However, when parents understand developmental stages and age-appropriate behavior, they understand why all discipline should be kind and firm (to maintain dignity and respect) instead of punitive (which produces doubt, shame, and guilt). It will be much easier for parents to use Positive Discipline methods—and they will save themselves a great deal of frustration—when they change their own attitudes based on knowledge. There are two beliefs that most parents share—and that must be changed before we can work effectively with very young children. Do you recognize either of these beliefs?

> When parents understand developmental stages and age-appropriate behavior, they understand why all discipline should be kind and firm (to maintain dignity and respect) instead of punitive (which produces doubt, shame, and guilt).

- The belief that you can control toddlers and make them "mind."
- The belief that children are intentionally trying to defeat you.

Because infants and toddlers are small and adults can easily pick them up and move them around, we are often seduced into believing that we can control their behavior. Think about this for a moment, though: Can any of us truly control another person's behavior? Feelings? Beliefs? It is often difficult enough for us to control our own! Instead of expecting to control young children, consider learning methods that invite cooperation. Abandoning the mistaken notion of control and working toward cooperation may save your dignity and sanity—and that of your children!

The cooperative child you envision living with five years from now is being shaped and encouraged each moment of every day. By contrast, the toddler you swat, scold, and scoop up from the pile of books she pulled out of the bookcase is likely to become the six-year-old who refuses to pick up her toys, clothes, and shoes—and the teenager who slips out the bedroom window after you've grounded her for the month. The toddler who is gently redirected to the pot and pan cupboard without punishment is learning to cooperate. Your requests for her cooperation in clearing up a mess when she is a first-grader will have a much greater chance of meeting with success.

> Can any of us truly control another person's behavior? Feelings? Beliefs? It is often difficult enough for us to control our own! Instead of expecting to control young children, consider learning methods that invite cooperation.

You will know that children aren't trying to defeat you when you understand developmental stages and age-appropriate behavior. An eighteen-month-old who plows ahead toward the forbidden bookcase has no intention of defying you. He sees something new, colorful, and interesting. He wants to experience it. Nowhere in his mind is there even a fragment of thought regarding you, your rules, or possible safety issues (well, maybe a fragment, but only a very fleeting one). When adults use their own thinking perspective to interpret a situation, they assign adult values to children's behavior. "He's just defying my word!" is adult thinking, not your child's intention. Once we as adults realize this, it becomes far easier to respond without anger, punishment, or our own worrisome fear that we are bad parents when our young children "don't mind." We'll take another look at this as we explore every toddler's favorite word: "No!"

What Does Your Toddler Really "Know" About "No"?

CHILDREN UNDER THE age of three do not understand "no" in the way most parents think they do (and a full understanding of "no"

Over and over, we hear this question:
"How do I make my toddler mind?"
The following, from the mother of the
"Energizer Bunny," is typical.

Q. I have a seventeen-month-old son who is into everything, sometimes things that are dangerous. He climbs on everything, opens everything, and pushes the buttons on anything and everything he can find. Are there positive ways I can get him to stop his dangerous activities? I tell him "No!" but he just smiles at me and keeps doing whatever he's doing. I slap his hand sometimes if he is near something dangerous. He is very determined and just keeps going back to the forbidden activity. I think he is the Energizer Bunny in disguise! Help!

A. Although your son's behavior is undoubtedly frustrating at times, you do have reason to celebrate. Your child is very normal. What he is doing is developmentally and age appropriate. Does it make sense to punish a child for doing what comes naturally? Your job as a parent is to supervise and make sure he doesn't do dangerous things, but please don't slap his hands and tell him no. Do childproof your home to eliminate as many dangerous things as possible. After that, distrac-

doesn't occur magically when the child turns three; it is a developmental process). "No" is an abstract concept that is in direct opposition to the developmental need of young children to explore their world and to develop their sense of autonomy and initiative.

Oh, your child may "know" you don't want her to do something. She may even know she will get an angry reaction from you if she does it. However, she cannot understand "why" in the way an adult thinks she can. Why else would a child look at you before doing what she knows she shouldn't do, grin, and do it anyway? Knowing things as a toddler means something far different than knowing

tion is the most effective parenting tool for this age. This means you kindly and firmly remove him from what he can't do and from what is dangerous, and show him what he can do—over and over.

It can be frustrating to deal with a persistent, independent toddler, but how wonderful that your child does not curb his need to develop autonomy in spite of your slaps and telling him no. Doubt and shame might be the lessons children learn from constant reprimands, repeated swats, and the frustration of limited access to all the tempting goodies surrounding them. Autonomy and initiative form the cornerstones of self-esteem. Doubt, shame, and guilt (however unintentionally created) are barriers to the growth of these healthy, necessary characteristics.

These stages of development do not mean children should be allowed to do anything they want. It does explain why all methods to gain cooperation should be kind and firm at the same time instead of controlling and/or punitive. This is a time of life when your child's personality is being formed, and you want your child to make decisions about himself or herself that say "I am competent. I can try, make mistakes, and learn. I am loved. I am a good person." If you are tempted to help your child learn by guilt, shame, or punishment, you will be creating discouraging beliefs that are difficult to reverse in adulthood.

things as an adult. Her version of knowing lacks the internal controls necessary to halt her roving fingers. Researchers including Jean Piaget discovered long ago that toddlers lack the ability to understand cause and effect (an excellent reason not to try to lecture and argue a toddler into doing what you want). In fact, higher-order thinking like understanding consequences and ethics may not develop until children are as old as ten.

Understanding Developmental and Age Appropriateness Offers Opportunities to Teach and Empower

REMEMBER THAT AROUND the ages of one through three, children enter the stage when they develop a sense of autonomy (as discussed in chapters 6 and 7). As we have discussed, this means it is a child's developmental job to explore and experiment. Can you imagine how confusing it is to a child to be punished for what he is developmentally programmed to do? He is faced with a real dilemma (at a subconscious level): "Do I obey my parents, or do I follow my biological drive to develop autonomy and skills by exploring and experimenting in my world?"

Supervision and Distraction

SAFETY IS AN important consideration during the first years of life, and your job is to keep your child safe without letting your fears discourage her. For this reason, supervision is an important parenting tool, along with kindness and firmness while redirecting or teaching your child.

Parents almost always cite the danger of a child running into the street as a justification for spanking a toddler. Reasons include the life-and-death nature of the situation, the need for immediate compliance, and the effectiveness of a spanking for "getting a child's attention." The thing they forget is that to a toddler, an angry, shouting, spanking parent is probably far more frightening than any street.

Even if parents believe punishment effectively "teaches" a two-year-old child not to run into the street, they would not let her play near a busy street unsupervised (as discussed in chapter 6). They know, spanking or no spanking, that they can't expect her to understand what she has "learned" well enough to have that responsibility.

Adults must be alert to danger, provide consistent and firm guidance, and be able to move very quickly! There is no substitute for supervision.

Redirection

AMONG THE MOST useful parenting tools for living with toddlers is redirection.

Thirteen-month-old Ellen was crawling rapidly toward the dog's dish—one of her favorite "toys"—when her dad spotted her. He called out her name firmly. Ellen paused and looked back over her shoulder. Her dad gathered her up and carried her across the room to where her barnyard set was waiting.

"Here, sweetie," he said with a tickle, "see what the pigs and cows are up to."

If Ellen chooses to head for the dog's dish again, her dad can intercept her and direct her toward a more acceptable object. Acting without lecturing or shaming avoids a power struggle and lets Ellen know that Dad won't let her play with the dish.

What if Ellen keeps returning to the forbidden dish? How many times must a parent redirect a child's attention? Well, as many times as it takes. As we've mentioned before, it takes patience and perseverance to train a young child. If Ellen's dad slapped her hand or spanked her, would she still want to play with the dish? Probably so. Even if spankings stop the behavior, what is the cost in loss of self-esteem? What are the lessons about violence? Kindly but firmly directing Ellen toward acceptable objects, and continuing to do so until she gets the message, guides her behavior without punishing or shaming and without inviting a battle of wills.

At Another Level:
The "Child Power" of "No"

TODDLERS ARE EXPERIENCING individuation, learning to see themselves as separate, independent beings. It's a natural and healthy

The following examples illustrate intellectual development and help us see why children can't understand some concepts (such as "no") as soon as adults think they can.

- Take two balls of clay that are the same size. Ask a three-year-old if they are the same. Make adjustments by taking clay from one ball and adding it to the other until the child agrees that they are the same size. Then, right in front of her, smash one ball of clay. Then ask her if they are still the same. She will say no and will tell you which one she thinks is bigger. A five-year-old will tell you they are the same and can tell you why.

- Find four glasses: two glasses that are of the same size, one glass that is taller and thinner, and one glass that is shorter and fatter. Fill the two

process, but one that is frequently trying for parents and teachers. At one level it doesn't take long for a young child to learn the power of the word "no" or that by using it he can provoke all sorts of interesting reactions. Adults can't always avoid these confrontations, but changing your own behavior and expectations can lessen their impact. There are actually three types of "no": the ones you can avoid saying, the ones you can avoid hearing, and the ones that you just learn to live with.

How Not to Say No

"SOMETIMES I LISTEN to myself talking to my two-year-old," one mom confided to a group of friends, "and all I hear myself saying is 'no' and 'don't.' I sound so negative, but I don't know what else to do." There are actually a number of ways adults can avoid saying the "no" word themselves.

glasses that are the same size with water until a three-year-old agrees they are the same. Then, right in front of her, pour the water from one of these glasses into the short, fat glass, and the other one into the tall, thin glass. Then ask her if they still hold the same amount of water. Again, she will say no and will tell you which glass she thinks contains the most water. A five-year-old will tell you they contain the same amount and can tell you why.

Both of these examples demonstrate thinking abilities identified by Piaget. When we understand that perceiving, interpreting, and comprehending an event are so markedly different for young children, our expectations as adults alter. The meaning children attach to their experiences does not match the meaning adults attach to the same experiences.

- *Say what you do want.* Elizabeth, who is three years old, is delightedly throwing blocks across the room. Her teacher walks in and immediately says, "No throwing blocks!" Now Elizabeth hears what not to do, but she may have a hard time figuring out what she *can* do. It might be more effective if her teacher says, "Blocks are for using on the floor" or "You look like you want to do some throwing. Would you like me to help you find a toy you can throw?" The next time you start to tell your child no, ask yourself what you want to have happen. Then tell your child what you want.

- *Say "yes" instead.* It's really very easy to say yes instead of no. Many parents are programmed to respond with an automatic no. When you are about to say no, try asking yourself, "Why not?" Take a look at eighteen-month-old Cindy. She is playing in the kitchen sink, splashing water everywhere, and having a wonderful time. When Mom enters the room, her first response is to grab Cindy and say, "Stop that!"

  But why? Cindy's eyes are sparkling; she is absorbed in the feel of the water and the magic of the droplets flying around. Her clothes can be changed, and she'll probably think it's a terrific game to help Mom mop the floor afterward. In other words, there may be no reason to say no this time. Mom and Cindy may be better off if they forget the "no" and simply enjoy themselves.

- *Try distraction and redirection.* Act firmly and calmly remove a child from the forbidden item. Refocus attention: "Let's see how many birds are at the bird feeder this morning."

- *Offer limited choices.* When your toddler demands a different cup for his juice, hold up the cup you gave him or offer to put the juice away until later. (Remember, toddlers may use their whole bodies to object, as in a tantrum. Just because little Jenny throws a tantrum doesn't mean that your handling of the situation was inappropriate. Tantrums happen.)

Next time, try offering a choice of two cups before pouring the juice.

How to Avoid Hearing the "No" Word

WHERE DO CHILDREN learn the word "no"? Obviously, from hearing their parents and caregivers say it so often. It is especially important to avoid saying no to children during the first three years of their lives. Remember, the word "no" can create real confusion—both psychologically and in brain development. It is developmentally appropriate for children to explore. When we say no we may be hampering normal development.

Again, this does not mean children should be able to do anything they want. It does mean that parents will encourage appropriate developmental stages and enhanced brain development when they use the methods described throughout this book with kindness and firmness.

When You Must Say No

WE DO NOT mean to imply that a parent should never say no. We must always teach before comprehension occurs. That is part of the learning process. We talk to children before they comprehend words, we remove them from things they can't do before they comprehend why, we hug and cuddle before they are able to hug back.

Real understanding—the ability to use a skill without consciously thinking about it—takes

> Remember, the word "no" can create real confusion—both psychologically and in brain development. It is developmentally appropriate for children to explore. When we say no we may be hampering normal development.

time, and sometimes it just feels good to say no! Providing kind and firm discipline and teaching developmentally appropriate boundaries is the destination, but we will make many mistakes along the way. However, since infants and toddlers do not really comprehend, saying no is effective only when used with other methods.

Teach with Your Actions

WITH CHILDREN FROM birth to age three, it is best to say no with actions instead of words. As Rudolf Dreikurs used to say, "Shut your mouth and act."

Nine-month-old Gabriel started biting his mother, Trina, while she was nursing. Trina immediately put him down and left the room. Gabriel howled. In about a minute, Trina came back and picked him up. The next time he took a bite, she repeated the process. Gabriel must have caught on, because he didn't go for a third bite.

Every time two-year-old Tanya started for the street, her father would quickly clasp her hand in his own. She would squirm, resist, and try to pull away. Dad held on. After a moment, she would continue, holding hands with Dad. He would let go after a few moments, only to repeat his action if she again headed for the street. Tanya soon stopped running into the street. One reason Dad's strategy was effective was that he did not say a word. (We don't know why words seem to invite a playful power struggle from toddlers and two-year-olds—but they do!) Actions do speak louder than words—and are much more effective when applied kindly and firmly.

> Actions do speak louder than words—and are much more effective when applied kindly and firmly.

When two-and-a-half-year-old Michael started a temper tantrum in the supermarket, his mother picked him up and took him to the car. She calmly held him firmly on her lap until he stopped screaming and writhing. They then went into the store and tried again. They made three trips to the car that day. The next time they went to the supermarket, they made only one trip to the car. The third time, Michael stopped crying as soon as his mother picked him up and headed for the car.

It was easier for these parents to act kindly and firmly because they understood developmental and age appropriateness. They knew it was normal for their children to test their autonomy and initiative in socially unacceptable or dangerous ways. Were they embarrassed when the other shoppers stared at them or suggested that their child "needed a good spanking"? Perhaps. They also knew that it is a parent's job to provide constant supervision at this age and to redirect misbehavior through kind and firm action. Parenting requires both patience and courage, and raising active, curious, energetic toddlers merits a medal of special honor. It is an awesome task.

Words and Action

INSTEAD OF EXPECTING your child to comprehend and "mind" when you say no, follow through with action. You might say "No biting" while gently cupping your hand over the child's mouth and removing her from biting range. You might say "No hitting" while removing him and showing him what he *can* do. The "no" may be more for your benefit than the child's—it helps you create the energy you need for kind and firm action.

A Hugging No

WE SAW A delightful cartoon that depicted a mother shouting "No!" to her toddler. The child shouted back, "Yes!" The mother shouted louder, "No!" The child screamed, "Yes!" Then the mother obviously remembered the importance of being kind and firm at the same time. She knelt down, gave her child a hug and softly said, "No." The little boy said, "Okay."

Saying no is fine when you understand what your child does and does not understand. The frustration occurs when parents think the word "no" by itself is enough to create obedience.

We know that parents don't mean to create doubt and shame in their children, nor do they mean to harm their self-esteem. Yet that is often what happens when parents do not understand developmentally appropriate behavior.

> We know that parents don't mean to create doubt and shame in their children, nor do they mean to harm their self-esteem. Yet that is often what happens when parents do not understand developmentally appropriate behavior.

The "No" We Want Children to Say

CHILDREN NEED TO learn to say no. Most two-year-olds seem to accomplish this task with relish. The good news is that saying no is a valuable life skill. This toddler will one day grow into a teenager who will be faced with offers of drugs, alcohol, and other dangerous options. When these choices loom, we want our young adult to say no. Right now, when his entire vocabulary seems to consist of only that word, we are not so thrilled.

Give children chances to say no in appropriate ways. "Do you want some juice?" A "no" response to juice is perfectly acceptable. Or you might ask, "May Auntie give you a hug before she leaves?" Because children need to have some control over their bodies, the answer of "no" ought to be an option, one that hopefully Auntie can accept without offense.

Developmental Clocks May Vary

EACH HUMAN BEING is a work of art. Look at the variety we see in appearance alone: skin color, hair color and texture, shape of the nose, color of the eyes, height, weight, shape—each one of us is unique. And physical characteristics are only the beginning of our uniqueness.

Do you recognize any of these parenting fantasies that thrive when parents lack understanding about developmental appropriateness?

1. Believing that your child should listen to you and do what you say.
2. Believing that your toddler understands when you say no and can learn to be obedient.
3. Hoping your child will be "good" because you are tired and don't want to be bothered.

What is the truth?

1. Toddlers are too busy following their developmental blueprint to do what you say—most of the time.
2. "No" is an abstract concept that cannot be understood by toddlers in the way parents think they can understand.
3. Children are always "good," but they are not always obedient—especially during the development of autonomy.

Temperament, as we have discovered, is as individual as a fingerprint. So is the rate at which we develop and grow. Understanding developmental appropriateness—the sorts of things children do, think, and are capable of at different stages—can help parents and teachers work effectively with children just as they are at the moment.

Windows of Opportunity

CHILDREN ARE, in many ways, similar. Johnny and Mary, for instance, will both be learning to walk in the first year and a half of life. But children are different, too. Mary doggedly pulled herself along the furniture and took her first steps at ten months of age, while Johnny was contentedly crawling at eleven months. By thirteen months of age, both children were walking, exploring their world on their own two feet. Similar, yet unique!

Picture a window in your mind. Although the window is framed on all sides, there is a great deal of space in the middle. In the same way, many behaviors and early experiences in our children's lives take place in just such a window. The window for getting a first tooth can be anywhere from six to ten months of age. There are similar windows for physical, intellectual, and emotional development, and each child has his or her own individual schedule, neither exactly like nor completely unlike anyone else's.

Very few things in the world of parenting come in only black or white. This book is all about choices, windows, and possibilities. Understanding your child's individual progress—her development of trust, autonomy, and initiative, her temperament, her physical development—will help you make the best choices for her and for you. Let's take a look at one way developmental stages influence your child's perceptions and behavior.

> Very few things in the world of parenting come in only black or white. This book is all about choices, windows, and possibilities.

Process Versus Product

IT'S A BUSY Friday evening, and you're off on a quick trip to the grocery store with your toddler. You have a definite goal in mind, namely to grab the necessary ingredients for dinner in time to get home, prepare and eat it, and still be on time for your older son's soccer game. For you, going to the store means obtaining the desired *product*. For your toddler, however, the product just isn't the point. Children are firmly rooted in the here and now; they think and experience life differently than adults do. A trip to the store is all about the *process*—the smells, the colors, the feelings, the experience. Being sandwiched into a busy schedule just doesn't allow time to enjoy the process!

Children do not share our goal-oriented expectations. It isn't always possible to go along with a child's relaxed approach, either. Sometimes we really do need to run in, grab the chicken, and run home again. But being aware of your child's tendency to focus on process rather than product can help you provide a balance. There may be times when you can take a leisurely browse through the store, enjoying the flowers in the floral department and the magazines in the rack or smelling the fragrant peaches and naming colors together. Children are miniature Zen masters, able to focus on the moment and enjoy it—an ability many adults would do well to learn.

When you must hurry, take time to explain to your child why you must shop quickly this time. You can explain that you want him to hold your hand and that you will have to walk past the toys and other interesting things. You can offer to let him help you find the chicken and carry it to the checkout stand. Then you will walk back to the car and drive home. Helping a child understand clearly what is expected and what will happen makes it more likely he will cooperate with you.

The Joy of Understanding Your Child

PARENTS OFTEN SAY in their more frazzled moments, "I can hardly wait until my child is two—or three, or ten, or twenty-one." Remaining patient, kind, and firm requires effort and energy that may be in short supply sometimes. But we cannot turn the clock ahead, and when we take time to enjoy our children, we won't want to. We and our toddlers are in the here and now of their personal developmental timelines. There are important lessons to be learned and tasks to be accomplished—and there are no shortcuts.

No one said parenting would be easy. However, it can bring more joy than frustration when you understand developmental and age-appropriate behavior and know effective parenting skills.

No one said par-enting would be easy. However, it can bring more joy than frustration when you understand devel-opmental and age-appropriate behavior and know effective parenting skills.

After her parenting class on developmental appropriateness, Lisa reported to her classmates, "I sure do have a happier home since I stopped yelling at Melissa. The things she does that used to make me angry are now fascinating to me. I think she'll get an A in autonomy. I will also get an A in kind and firm distraction because I'm getting lots of practice!"

PART FOUR

Sleeping, Eating, and Toileting

You Can't Make 'Em Do It

Gather any group of parents with very young children together and, inevitably, the conversation will turn in one of three directions. "I can't get my little girl to take a nap," one mom complains. "She's up all day, then she falls asleep early in the evening. That would be great if she stayed asleep—but she wakes up at three in the morning and wants to play. How can I get her to sleep when we do?"

"My son sleeps fine," a dad says, "but he absolutely refuses to have anything to do with his potty seat. He's almost three; my mother says her kids were all trained by the age of two. We're starting to panic."

"Well, we're still on the basics," another mom adds sadly. "My little boy thinks he can live on hot dogs and Cheerios, with an occasional cookie thrown in. I've bribed and coaxed and argued, but he just clamps his lips together when I offer him anything else. I dread mealtimes."

Most of us can relate to these beleaguered parents; in fact, you may be nodding your head as you read this. Sleeping, eating, and toileting seem to become battles in most families. Who starts these wars? And why?

We believe that like any other parenting battle, the sleeping, eating, and toileting wars are based on fear and a lack of understanding and cooperation skills. What do parents fear? Usually, whether we realize it or not, what we fear is losing control (something we never really have at all). We may believe we're being permissive or that we're allowing children to be the boss. We may fear that our children will be savages if we don't "tame" them, or that somehow our precious children won't fit the myth of the perfect child and that others will think less of them—and of us.

Understanding developmental and age appropriateness will help you work with your child as he masters his body. Learning cooperation skills will help, too—especially when you face the reality that sleeping, eating, and toileting are three areas where your child is in complete control. It is, after all, his body!

Throughout this book we will repeat the idea that it takes two to have a power struggle, because it is one that so many parents either do not understand or quickly forget: You can't make your children sleep; you can't make them eat; you can't make them use the toilet. However, there are ways to invite cooperation—as long as your methods are respectful of developmental and age appropriateness.

All humans must sleep and eat to survive. Toileting is a bodily need that has social significance. None of these functions becomes a battleground unless it becomes more important for a child (or a parent) to "win" than to do what comes naturally. The key is for parents to learn to support cooperation instead of inviting power struggles.

Eating, sleeping, and toileting take up much of the first three years of children's lives. All three will be easier if parents and caregivers remember these basic considerations:

• Readiness

  Is this developmentally appropriate? Is the timing right for my child? Am I ready, too?

(continued on next page)

- Weaning

  Is this a habit? What is the best way to let go—for myself and for my child? Letting go is difficult but necessary for both of us.

- Control

  As they do with sleeping and eating, adults set the stage for children to succeed in toilet training. Ultimately it is up to the child to eat what, when, and how much she chooses. Falling asleep (or staying awake) is a child's responsibility. And each child will master his own bladder and bowel functions on his own timetable.

  The truth is that we can offer support and training, set the stage for success, and learn to let go. But we can't make 'em do it!

10

Sleeping

"I'm Not Tired"

MOST BABIES SPEND more time asleep than awake during the first few months of their lives. Many power struggles over sleeping as your child grows can be avoided if you help your child learn to get to sleep by herself as early in her life as possible. This means putting her in her crib just before she falls asleep. (We know this isn't always possible with tiny babies who doze off after a few sucks on the bottle or breast. However, be aware of habits that may be forming.)

Desperate, sleep-deprived parents usually want to be sure that their demanding infants will sleep—right now! Many parents find they are afraid to lay down a drowsy or sleeping baby for fear of waking her. But waking up and being allowed to go back to sleep after a little fussing works fine. You can add a gentle pat on the back to soothe her back to sleep.

"But isn't it just easier to hold her while she sleeps and get a few moments of quiet for myself?" you may be asking. Adults often try to take responsibility for getting the baby to sleep and then managing the environment to keep him asleep ("Shh! The baby is *asleep!*"

they anxiously stage-whisper), then feel guilty, frustrated, or annoyed when they fail to ensure uninterrupted snooze time. Parents can make an effort to learn what works best for each child: we can explore the relative virtues of darkness versus night-lights, music versus silence, warm rooms versus cool ones. But *sleeping is the baby's job.* We invite a battle when we try to make his sleep our responsibility. (We discuss the "family bed" on page 136.)

SLEEPING SINGLE

Q. My two daughters (twelve months and almost three years old) will not fall asleep by themselves. I have to lie down with them until they fall asleep. Usually I fall asleep, too, and the whole evening is shot. Actually, the whole bedtime routine is a battle. They scream about having a bath, getting into their jammies, and going to bed. My older daughter tells me she isn't tired. I try to convince her that she is. When I finally get them to bed and read a story, they cry for more. I'm a stay-at-home mom, so my children get plenty of attention—but it never seems to be enough. Help!

A. When children sleep with you, they are not learning "I am capable." Parents usually suffer more than their children do while helping their children learn they can go to sleep by themselves. Are you willing to suffer to help your child? Believe me, letting them cry it out will be much harder for you than for them.

There are two main ingredients for success in helping your children learn to go to sleep by themselves:

1. Your understanding that this is the most loving thing you can do for your children. It is not helpful to teach them, even inadvertently, that they are not capable except to manipulate others.

2. Your confidence. They will feel this from your energy and from your body language. Energy is very readable. Children feel safe and trusting when

Some babies are born with more active temperaments, while others may have colic or other physical problems. These infants may require more holding and comforting during the first three to six months until you (and your doctor) know your baby well enough to know if the problems are physical or not. Establish good sleeping habits as soon as you feel confident that your child does not have any physical problems.

parents are confident. When you are confident, it will be easier for you to be kind and firm.

We suggest you put the children in separate bedrooms. They will probably cry for three to five nights until they get used to the fact that you know what is best for them and that you are going to stick to your resolve with confidence. Use your intuition to decide if you want to help them learn cold turkey or in stages, by going in to let them know you are there (according to the Ferber theory), but not lying down, cuddling, or coddling. Our thinking is that visiting your child's room while she cries may be teasing. (We question whether a baby knows the difference between five minutes and five hours. The important thing is that they experience consistency in finding you every morning.) In either case, parents who go cold turkey and parents who go in for a few seconds of comfort after five minutes, then ten minutes, then fifteen minutes, and so on agree that it takes three to five days for children to learn to fall asleep by themselves.

Your children receive plenty of love during the day and they see you every morning. We do not believe they will feel unloved or abandoned if they have to cry for a while as they learn to fall asleep by themselves, and it is actually empowering and loving to teach children the skills they will need to become healthy, responsible people. Remember, it is not your job to fix every problem for your children. How will they learn they can solve problems if they aren't allowed opportunities to try?

Creating a More Peaceful Bedtime

MOST PARENTS AND children will wrestle with bedtime at some point during their journey together. Here are some ideas that may help you make bedtime a highlight in your day—and keep battles to a minimum:

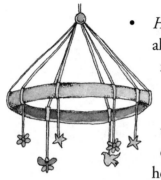

- *Have your child help you create a bedtime routine chart.* List all of the things you do before sleep time. Find pictures in magazines or draw pictures to represent each task. Make this fun: decorate your chart with glitter, markers, and stickers, then post it in a prominent spot. Now the routine chart becomes the boss. Your child can't manipulate a chart—and will be less inclined to try when it's something he helped create. Start the bedtime routine by getting him involved. Ask him to show you what is next on the chart.

- *Teach your child to brush her own teeth.* Some dentists insist that parents brush their children's teeth for them even past the preschool years. They may not realize that this often creates power struggles that make children resistant to brushing their teeth. If toothbrushing starts to look more like body wrestling, use methods that are more likely to invite cooperation.

  The most important job is to teach children the habit of brushing their teeth. You can teach her how to do a good job, but don't expect it. Try a toothbrushing party where all family members brush together. Focus on serving non-sugary foods—it might prove a better tooth decay battle strategy than aiming a toothbrush at that tiny face.

- *You may want to play "Let's Pretend" to prepare your child for what is going to happen.* It's usually wise to do this before bedtime arrives, perhaps during a moment of play together during the day. Try role-playing going to bed crying and going to bed happy. You might want to show her what each one looks like, and then let her do it. Remember, this exercise is intended to teach. Pretend she is getting her jammies on. Tell her you have faith in her to do it. Let her know that if she cries, you will go to the bathroom. Let her pretend she is coming to knock on the door to tell you she is ready because she has her jammies on and has chosen a book to read. You can even pretend to be the child and let her be the parent. Model cooperation for her, and have some fun doing it (no one ever said parenting had to be boring).

- *If your child says, "I don't want to go to bed," don't respond.* Children throw out sparks. By responding, we feed the flame until it becomes a bonfire. It doesn't help to tell her she is tired or cranky or to try to talk her into feeling sleepy. That invites argument—a surefire recipe for a power struggle. In a power struggle, if one participant wins, the other loses. In this case, though, you both lose because you are exhausted and frustrated by the time you get her to do what she needs to do. It is your job to step out of the power struggle and create a win/win solution. Just continue, kindly and firmly, with the routine. Ask, "What is next on your chart?"

> If your child says, "I don't want to go to bed," don't respond. Children throw out sparks. By responding, we feed the flame until it becomes a bonfire.

- *If your child is old enough to manage, don't put his jammies on for him.* Children feel capable when they can do things for themselves (remember, two- and three-year-olds are working on autonomy and initiative). When parents and caregivers do too much for them, they learn "I'm only capable of making other people take care of me." If your child objects, crossing his arms and jutting out his chin, kindly say, "I know you can do it. Come get me when you have your jammies on and have picked out the book you want to read." Then go to the bathroom until he

knocks on the door to tell you he is ready. (He will be prepared for this and will know what to do if you have played
"Let's Pretend" as described above.) You might want to let
him set a timer to see how quickly he can get his jammies on.

- *If you have more than one child, decide whether you want them
  to go to bed at the same time or at separate times.* It probably
  won't take as long as you fear to do two routines when you
  combine part of the routines for both children. For instance,
  you may decide to have bath time and playtime together.
  The other parent can play with your older child while you
  get the baby in her jammies. Or your older child can help
  you by playing with the baby while you change her diapers.
  It might help her feel special to help instead of fighting.
  This could create a sense of belonging and significance
  that will help her become more cooperative about going
  to bed.

- *Decide on one book or two, then stick to the agreement.* Don't
  get involved in a debate. Children learn the most from kind
  and firm actions. You might say, "It is time to tell me the
  happiest and saddest thing that happened to you today." If
  she keeps begging for one more story, give her a kiss good
  night and leave the room. Yes, she may cry, but your kind,
  respectful action will teach her that manipulation is not an
  option.

- *Give a big hug—and leave.* Remember, the more confident
  you are, the easier it will be for your children.

Trust yourself to modify these suggestions to fit your style; you
may want to add prayers, a song, or some other special item to your
routine chart. Bedtime may be difficult sometimes, but you can feel
confident that you are helping your children learn to go to sleep by
themselves—and building confidence and self-esteem for them in
the process.

Does It Work?

TARA LEVINE TRIED *one more time to stuff her small son's arm into his pajama sleeve and gave up in frustration as he wailed and wriggled free again. Ever since baby Sean had been born, bedtime had meant a battle with two-year-old Tyler. Tara knew that children sometimes struggled with the addition of a new sibling to the family and she thought she and Miles, her husband, had prepared Tyler well.*

Ever since Sean had come home from the hospital, however, Tyler had refused to fall asleep without a parent in his bed. He woke up several times a night, and he resisted the whole bedtime process. Tara sighed and picked up the pajama top again. Tomorrow, she resolved, she would dig out the notes from her parenting class. It was time to declare a cease-fire in the bedtime wars.

The next morning was Saturday. Tara waited until Sean was napping, then called Tyler to her side. "I have an idea," she said with a smile. "I need some help remembering how to do bedtime with you. Could you help me make a chart so we can remember everything we're supposed to do?"

Tyler liked being consulted by his mom and agreed to help, watching curiously as Tara gathered poster board, markers, magazines, and stickers.

"Now," she said, uncapping a marker, "what's the first thing we do at bedtime?"

Working together, Tara and her small son listed the bedtime tasks and illustrated each one with a picture. When the chart was complete, Tara wrote "Tyler's Bedtime Routine" in big letters and helped him sprinkle glitter on squiggly lines of glue. Tyler dashed off to show his creation to his dad.

Miles admired the bright chart, amused by his son's enthusiasm, but he looked dubiously at Tara. "I don't know," he said. "How can that make a difference?"

Miles and Tara were both surprised when the chart worked. Tara could hardly wait to share the results with her parenting group.

"Tyler still doesn't want to go to bed sometimes," she said, "but when he knows I mean it he immediately asks, 'Where's my chart?' We have to follow every step in order and he corrects me if I make a mistake. I tried to read only one book last night and Tyler reminded me that the chart says he gets two. He's been falling asleep without a whimper and sleeping through the night almost every night. His grandpa was so charmed by the bedtime chart that he asked if he could keep it as a memento after Tyler has outgrown it!"

It is wise to remember that nothing works all the time for all children but most toddlers thrive on routine, consistency, and encouragement. You may be surprised at how well your own toddlers respond.

Sleeping with Parents

MANY PARENTS WONDER whether or not they should let their children sleep with them. There are differing opinions on this issue. Books have been written about the "family bed" and the benefits of allowing children to sleep with their parents. Some people believe children feel more loved and secure when they sleep in their parents' bed. Other experts believe children become demanding and dependent when they sleep with their parents and that children have the opportunity to learn more cooperation, self-confidence, and autonomy when they sleep in their own beds. You can consider both sides, then decide what fits your family.

The first thing to consider is whether it works for you. Some parents find it very difficult to sleep when their children are in bed with them. Some couples find it greatly hampers their relationship (emotional and sexual). Many couples enjoy getting into bed to have a conversation, quietly read a book, and/or make love before going to sleep. (We purposely left out watching television, which can create a bigger wedge in a relationship than children in the bed.)

The second thing to consider is whether it works for your children. Does it help or hinder their development of autonomy, self-confidence, and self-reliance, or does it increase their sense of doubt and shame? We don't claim to have the answer. We do believe that educated parents will be more aware of what is happening in their child's world. Educated parents will be able to sense when their child becomes demanding or develops too much dependence (instead of healthy independence). Whichever choice you make, be sure that both adults agree. If you are a single parent, you may want to consider the implications of a new partner entering the picture and how committed you might wish to remain to sharing your bed with an infant, toddler, or preschooler.

Alfred Adler, a pioneer in the field of families and children's behavior, believed that children should not sleep in their parents' bed because it hampers their striving for self-confidence and invites children to believe themselves incapable of the independence that eventually leads to cooperation and interdependence. He also believed that there is a strong connection between daytime misbehavior and nighttime misbehavior—in other words, children who create difficulties during the day would also create difficulties at night.

Adler told the following story about a woman who came to him with a "problem" child. After hearing the woman's complaints about her problems with the child during the day, Adler asked, "How does the child behave during the night?" The woman replied, "I don't have any problems at night." This surprised Adler because of his theory that daytime and nighttime behavior are related. After a bit more discussion, Adler asked again, "Are you sure you don't have any problems during the night?" The woman assured him, "Oh no, I don't have any problems at night." Finally Adler guessed what might be happening at night. He asked, "Where does the child sleep?" The woman replied, "Why she sleeps with me, of course."

Adler explained to the woman that the sleeping arrangement was part of the problem. Of course the child was not creating any problems at night, because her inappropriate demands were being met. During the day the child was only trying to get the same level of attention she received at night, and she created problems when her mother did not cater to her as she did at night.

If your child is sleeping in your bed and is very demanding and dependent during the day, you might want to start the weaning process. As H. Stephen Glenn and Jane Nelsen point out in their book, *Raising Self-Reliant Children in a Self-Indulgent World,* "Weaning has never been easy for the weanor or the weanee, but it is necessary for the survival of both."

Some parents don't allow their children to sleep with them during the night but welcome them into their bed on weekend mornings for "morning snuggles." Other parents have a routine of lying down on their children's beds for story time. They make it clear to their children that they will leave when the story is over. They want to avoid the habit many children quickly adopt of insisting their parents stay in their bed until after they fall asleep.

Again, use your wisdom to decide what works best for you and your children. Few things are always wrong; many parents find that allowing a child to snuggle in their bed is the best cure for occasional fears and nightmares—or the best time for quiet confidences. If you are weighing your own needs against the skills your child will eventually need to develop, chances are excellent that you'll make the right choice.

> If you are weighing your own needs against the skills your child will eventually need to develop, chances are excellent that you'll make the right choice.

Weaning

"WHAT IF IT is too late?" you may be asking. "I have already allowed these habits to develop and my child is now very demanding. She won't go to sleep at all unless I lie down with her or let her sleep with us. When I try to break her of the habit, she screams—and I can't stand it. I always give in. It has created all the problems you have discussed, but I can't stand to listen to her cry."

Knowing in advance that weaning is difficult helps—but only a little. Here are some tips to help you survive the weaning process.

- *Give up your "guilt button."* Children know when they can push that button; they also know when it is gone. (Don't ask us how they know—they just do!) Guilt is rarely a positive, helpful feeling. Knowing why you are doing something will help you do what is necessary for the ultimate good of your child.

- *Tell your child what you are going to do.* Even if your child is preverbal, he or she will understand the feeling tone behind the words. A little warning and time to prepare will help both of you avoid unpleasant surprises and misinterpretation.

- *Follow through.* If you say it, mean it; and if you mean it, follow through with action that is kind and firm.

- *Hang in there.* If you've followed the first three steps, it usually takes at least three days for your child to believe that you mean what you say. This means that she will try very hard to get you to maintain the old habit. She will probably cry (or scream) for at least three nights. The crying time usually gets shorter each night, especially if you have followed the first tip.

- *Take time during the day for lots of hugs and other special time with your child.* Make sure this isn't "guilt penance" time but time for reassurance and enjoyment of your love for each other.

Allowing a child to "cry it out" is always a dilemma for parents. They wonder if this will be a traumatic event that will scar their child for life. We believe it is more traumatic for children to develop the belief of "I'm not capable," which may happen if they don't learn independence in small doses.

The more confidence you have in your decision, the easier it will be for your child to recover from the disappointment of not getting his way. It is important to remember that children do not always know what is best for them.

Sometimes adults don't get what they want—and sometimes they, too, have temper tantrums! However, they soon recover and life goes on. The more confidence you have in your decision, the easier it will be for your child to recover from the disappointment of not getting his way. It is important to remember that children do not always know what is best for them. The baby bird does not enjoy being pushed out of the nest, but the mother bird knows it is essential.

Bedtime hassles are common, and most families survive them. A little thought and planning may ease the process for you and for your children.

11

Eating

"Don't *Like* That!"

FOOD IS NOT only something we humans need to survive but something most of us enjoy. (In fact, some of us enjoy it a bit too much!) So why do mealtimes become such a struggle for the parents of so many toddlers?

Eating is a process entirely controlled by the person doing it. Even if you manage to squeeze, poke, or slide a bit of unwanted food between your child's lips, can you make him chew it? Swallow it? If you've ever tried, you undoubtedly know the answer. Let's explore when and why the battles begin.

Eating begins when you offer an infant a bottle or the breast. Adults often argue over which is "better." We encourage every mother to get as much information about the advantages and/or disadvantages of both methods and then to choose the one with which she feels most comfortable. It is our goal to support parents in managing their choices without any power struggles.

In spite of the many nutritional and emotional benefits of nursing, it is not mandatory. Many emotionally and physically healthy babies have been raised on formula and baby food. The key is to have knowledge about what you are doing and to have confidence in your choice. Remember that a confident mother is better able to foster a sense of trust in her baby. Either choice, bottle or breast, can supply the nurture an infant needs; both must eventually come to an end.

I n spite of the many nutritional and emotional benefits of nursing, it is not mandatory. Many emotionally and physically healthy babies have been raised on formula and baby food. The key is to have knowledge about what you are doing and to have confidence in your choice.

Babies are programmed by nature and their own reflexes to suck for nourishment and comfort, and they usually want to eat frequently. There are many different opinions about how to satisfy this basic need. The debate centers on breast-feeding, bottles, and formula. Not too many years ago, many doctors discouraged breast-feeding because formula, the product of science, was believed to be better. Now we understand that babies benefit in many ways from their mother's milk. Whichever choice you make, adapting to your baby's needs can be challenging.

In the following section, Jane, one of the authors (and mother of seven children), shares her nursing story and what it taught her about trusting her own instincts. It demonstrates many important aspects about a parent and child's early experiences with issues surrounding eating.

Nursing

HOW I WISH *I'd had more information on nursing from the beginning; I wouldn't have created so much pain for myself and my children as I learned. My first child was born in 1956 during the time when doctors were advocating a strict feeding schedule of every four hours. I didn't even question their reasoning. I just assumed they must know what they were talking about. Baby Terry would nurse and fall asleep. Often, during the afternoon, he would wake up after an hour and start crying. I would think, "Oh no! Three more hours before he can nurse." I would walk the floor with him and try to comfort him, but he would just cry until he was screaming. I tried pacifiers and water. They might work for a few minutes, but soon he would be screaming again. (It is painful for me to even remember this.)*

Finally, after two hours, I would "cheat" and nurse him before the four hours were up. He was so exhausted from crying that he would nurse for a minute or two and then fall asleep. How could I have been so ignorant that I didn't know he couldn't get enough in two minutes? I was so intimidated by the doctor's advice that I didn't think. I just assumed that I had to wait another four hours. Terry would wake up hungry in about an hour and we would go through another agonizing two hours before I would "cheat" again.

Because of my lack of information about nursing, I believed many myths. I believed that if my breasts weren't engorged, I didn't have any milk, that my milk must not be rich enough because it wasn't "milky white," and that Terry cried because I didn't have enough milk. The truth was that he cried because he wasn't nursing long enough to get enough nourishment and to build up my milk supply in the process. Another mistake was introducing him to cereal at two weeks (based on my doctor's suggestion) to fill him up. I didn't know that would only keep him from nursing long enough to build up my milk supply. I gave up in frustration after three weeks and put him on a bottle.

I tried nursing with my next three children—Jimmy, Kenny, and Brad—and even though I didn't wait four hours between each feeding, I still believed they needed cereal, apple juice, and baby food and that I didn't have enough milk unless I was engorged. I gave up after a few weeks each time, thinking my milk just wasn't good enough.

When my fifth child, Lisa, was born, I tried nursing again. I was on my way to failure once more when my sister-in-law told me about La Leche League and their book, The Womanly Art of Breastfeeding. *She told me there was no such thing as bad mother's milk, that engorgement wasn't a sign of "enough" milk, and that I should throw away all the formula bottles and supplemental foods and just nurse whenever my baby wanted to in order to build up my milk supply. I read the book, threw away the bottles and solid foods, and began a successful nursing experience.*

I don't know when I have ever been happier! I loved nursing on demand. There were times when Lisa would sleep five or six hours. In the late afternoon and evening she would sometimes nurse as often as every hour—or sometimes every fifteen minutes! By the time she was three and a half months old, she had regulated herself to a three-hour schedule during the day and would sleep through the night, even without cereal to "fill her up."

The Womanly Art of Breastfeeding answered so many questions that it became my bible. I became confident that Lisa didn't need supplemental foods; many babies don't until they're six months to one year old. Every month, my pediatrician would tell me I could introduce a new baby food, and I would just smile. The next month he would ask me if I had introduced the foods, and I would tell him I hadn't. He would suggest that maybe I should, just to make sure she didn't get anemic (iron is the only thing missing from mother's milk, although the baby is usually born with a year's supply of iron). I would ask him if he would like to take a blood test to see if she was in danger of anemia. He would say, looking sheepish, "I can tell from looking at her that she isn't anemic." He really was a wonderful doctor whom I trusted for the health care of my baby; I just knew that he didn't know as much as I did about nursing.

Most mothers find they occasionally have questions about nursing, feeding, bottles, and their babies' nutritional needs. One of the wisest things mothers can do is to begin right away to build a support and resource network. Many hospitals and maternity centers offer breast-feeding support; in fact, some even offer twenty-four-hour phone lines to call when you have questions. Churches, child care centers, and pediatricians may have information on new mothers' support groups, which can be invaluable in answering questions and boosting your confidence. Remember, no question is ever "stupid." Ask for help when you need it, and have confidence in your own wisdom and growing knowledge of *your* baby.

PULLING HAIR WHILE NURSING

Q. I know my eight-month-old daughter is too young for much active discipline, but I'm concerned that her roughness will become ingrained as a habit and I won't be able to alter it gently in the future. She's extremely active, energetic, and highly sensitive. She has been hitting, gouging, and yanking hair for a few weeks now, usually when nursing. I've tried taking hold of her arm and demonstrating how to be "gentle" (while reinforcing the idea with words) over and over, but I don't seem to be making any progress. Our poor cats are at their wits' end, as she yanks on them, too! Does anyone have any ideas, or is it too early to worry about this sort of thing (just another phase, that is)?

A. Please read the section in chapter 9 about what your child really knows about "no." This will help you to understand why supervision and distraction (over and over) are about the only things that are effective at this age—at least regarding the cats. When she pulls your hair while nursing, however, it can be effective to immediately (kindly and firmly) put her down and walk out of the room for about one minute. Then try nursing again. She may cry for that minute, but children this age learn more from kind and firm action than from words. Happy Nursing!

Introducing Solid Foods and Supplemental Bottles

EVENTUALLY ALL CHILDREN are ready to be weaned from bottle or breast and to move on to other foods. Jane continues with her own experience:

Introducing solid foods to Lisa was easy. When she was seven months old, we occasionally offered her some mashed banana or mashed potato. I might blend other fruits or vegetables in a blender with some liquid. I say "might" because sometimes we did and sometimes we didn't. We didn't feel any pressure, because we knew she was getting all she needed from breast milk during the first year. We saved a fortune (at least, it seemed like a fortune to us) on what we would have spent on formula and baby food. By the time she was one year old, she could eat many of the foods we cooked for our own meals if we mashed, chopped, or blended them for her to eat.

Babies often thrive on nursing for the first year. However, if you plan to be away from your baby (and an occasional night away is good for your own mental and emotional health, as well as your spouse's), it is easier if she is comfortable taking a bottle.

I made the mistake of not introducing my last baby to a bottle until I needed to leave her with a baby-sitter when she was three months old. It took me three days of almost constantly pushing a bottle of apple juice in her mouth before she would finally take it.

La Leche League suggests expressing (that is, pumping) breast milk into a bottle and freezing it (it looks like milky dishwater) so it is available when the mother will need to be away from the baby. This can allow Dad the opportunity to take turns with night feedings or other much needed "mommy breaks." Expressing breast milk also makes it possible for nursing to continue when a mother returns to work and must place her child with a caregiver. With time and practice, parents will learn to gauge the needs of their baby. Some babies do well on a combination of nursing, formula, and solids; some babies never need anything but breast milk. Babies, like adults, are unique individuals. Patience and a bit of trial and error will help you learn to know your baby's requirements.

Weaning

LISA WEANED HERSELF by her first birthday; she simply refused to nurse any more. Many mothers believe weaning can't be that easy, but it can be if mothers are willing to watch for the signs of readiness in their babies. Somewhere between the tenth and twelfth month, many babies lose interest in nursing (or in taking a bottle). Many mothers ignore the signs and push the bottle or breast at the baby until they give in and start taking it again (unless they are as stubborn as Lisa). Mothers do this for one of two reasons: 1) They are not aware that a loss of interest during this window of time may be a natural phenomenon that indicates a readiness for weaning; and 2) mothers sometimes want their babies to keep taking the bottle because it is an easy way to calm them when they are fussy and/or to help them to go to sleep.

Keeping babies on the bottle or breast after they are ready to stop may squelch the first blossoming of their sense of autonomy. It is important to realize that once the window of readiness to wean passes, nursing or taking a bottle may become a habit instead of a need. (This distinction of habit versus need can help adults determine timing in many areas of development, not just nursing.)

Missing this opportunity for weaning isn't a traumatic, life-damaging experience. Many parents have been unaware of the signs of readiness for weaning and have allowed their children to develop the bottle or nursing habit. They have also learned (from hard experience) that weaning is more difficult when it has become a habit. We do survive, however, even if we miss this one factor that could increase autonomy a little and make weaning much easier.

Some people disagree with this point of view. We know people who advocate nursing children as old as six or eight years old. This may be "right" for some. Parents who are miserable with extended nursing need encouragement to follow

> Keeping babies on the bottle or breast after they are ready to stop may squelch the first blossoming of their sense of autonomy. It is important to realize that once the window of readiness to wean passes, nursing or taking a bottle may become a habit instead of a need.

what is right for them. As we have said before, parents will enjoy their role much more when they have the knowledge and the confidence to follow their hearts.

Weaning Is Difficult

AS WE'VE MENTIONED before, "Weaning is never easy for the weanee or the weanor, but it is necessary for the ultimate good of both." Weaning is part of the larger, lifelong process of letting go and is vital to helping children develop their full potential. Weaning (and letting go) should not be confused with abandonment. Children need a lot of loving support during the weaning process.

> Weaning is part of the larger, lifelong process of letting go and is vital to helping children develop their full potential.

When parents begin the weaning process and let go with love at developmentally appropriate times, children are encouraged to trust, to learn confidence, and to develop healthy self-esteem.

Betty's son, Ben, began preschool at age two and a half. He proudly carried his own lunch box to school with him. But his bravado turned to dismay when snack time came. He wanted his bottle, while everyone else was using cups. Ben's teacher soon realized the cause of his tearful whimpering. That afternoon, she spent some time discussing the situation with Betty. They agreed to allow Ben to use a bottle when he sat at the snack table and when he was lying down for his nap, but the rest of the time the bottle would be kept in the refrigerator. Also, the bottle would contain only water. This plan was relayed to Ben. At the same time, Betty decided to limit the contents of Ben's bottles at home to water. She chose not to reduce their availability, allowing him to use the bottle with fewer restrictions at home.

Several times over the next week, Ben tested his teacher to see if she would give him his bottle at other times of the day. The teacher was sympathetic, offered to hold or hug Ben if he wished, and reassured him that he could have his bottle at snack or rest time but held firm to the plan she had made with Betty. By the second week, Ben stopped asking for his bottle throughout the day. Within the month, he had lost interest in the bottle at other times as well.

Ben continued to use his bottle at home. When Betty saw how successfully the plan at school had worked, she set similar limits at home. After another week or two, she happily gathered up the forgotten bottles and packed them off to a charity program serving infants.

Betty and Ben's teacher used a gradual approach to weaning. Betty could have just refused to bring in any bottles, but Ben, his teacher, and his classmates might have had a much more stressful few weeks. In the end, Ben would have given up his bottle either way. Being firm does not mean that cold turkey is the only way to break lingering habits.

Extended Nursing

SOME PARENTS DO choose to delay the weaning process, allowing children to nurse well into their preschool years. There are at least two sides to the story of extended nursing. We encourage you to become educated and aware before you decide what works for you and your baby. La Leche League and other groups encourage nursing for as long as it feels right for the mother and her child. If you decide you want to nurse for an extended period of time, La Leche League offers classes and support. (The support can be very helpful, since many people will be critical.) If you choose to extend nursing, you will have more confidence if your decision is based on education and awareness. (The La Leche League can be reached at 800-525-3243.)

Avoiding Food Fights

"IF YOU DON'T eat your vegetables, you won't get any dessert!" "If you don't eat your oatmeal for breakfast, you'll get it for lunch!" "You are going to sit there and eat until you finish your dinner if it takes all night!" These parents seem to believe they can make a child eat. We have seen just as many kids demonstrate that you *can't* make them eat. We've known children to throw up, sneak food to the dog, glare at the oatmeal through breakfast, lunch, and dinner, and sit there all night—or at least until the parent gives up in despair.

Remember, insisting on a particular course of action or behavior is an invitation for most toddlers to engage in a power struggle. It may also be helpful to realize that it isn't usually necessary to force exact quantities of healthy foods down your child's throat. Unless he suffers from a metabolic disorder or requires a special medical diet, many pediatricians believe that over time (not necessarily in one meal or even one day), a young child will tend to choose the foods his body requires. A parent's task is to prepare and present healthy, nutritious foods; it is a child's task to chew and swallow. Of course, it doesn't hurt to add foods you know your child likes as well.

> Remember, insisting on a particular course of action or behavior is an invitation for most toddlers to engage in a power struggle.

Inviting Cooperation at Mealtimes

MOST PEOPLE WHO lived during the Depression report that battles about food and picky eating simply didn't happen. Parents didn't make a fuss when a child didn't want to eat because there often wasn't enough to go around. When children didn't get any mileage out of being picky or resistant, they ate what was available or went hungry.

In these days, when many of us have so much (and when, as research tells us, most of us eat out several times each week), it's easy to lose sight of the simplicity of eating. Some parents have been so thoroughly hooked by their demanding toddlers that they prepare two or three different meals for dinner: one menu for adults, peanut butter sandwiches for the preschooler, hot dogs for the toddler. Simply put, children do what works. If refusing to eat what Mom puts on the table gets them the meal of their choice (and the feeling of power that goes along with it), they'll continue to refuse family meals, harried parents will continue to prepare alternatives, and no one will enjoy mealtimes.

There are, however, any number of ways to invite cooperation and harmony at the table. As with so many other issues in early childhood, parents can decide what they will do, give up the notion of control, remain kind and firm—and teach children to be responsible, cooperative, and capable.

"Sounds too good to be true," you may be thinking. And in reality, there is no one simple answer to mealtime hassles. Children (like adults) sometimes just aren't hungry. Their food preferences change over time and they may not always want to eat on your schedule. Still, some of the following suggestions and ideas may help you keep food from becoming a fight in your family.

- *Don't force-feed.* Insisting that children eat particular foods in particular quantities at particular times will only create power struggles—and most parents of toddlers find they have lots of those already! If your baby spits food at you, it may be a clue that she's had enough. Don't insist on feeding more; get a sponge and teach her to mop up the mess. You may want to set an egg timer and let your child know that mealtime will end when the bell rings. Remove any uneaten food at that time, without shaming or lecturing.

  Good nutrition is important, but distasteful foods can sometimes be offered in tasty ways. Rather than forcing your child to stare at the egg congealing on his plate, use it to prepare French toast or a cheese-filled omelette. Fruits and some vegetables can be pureed and added to milk or yogurt, and a good multivitamin can fill in the gaps. Don't get hooked into preparing special meals or giving too many snacks because your toddler refused to eat; doing so will only reinforce his desire for special service and attention. Be kind and firm (yes, we know we sound like a broken record, but it works); serve healthy meals, include foods you know your toddler likes, and go with the flow.

- *Learn to know your child's needs and preferences.* Your little one may have no trouble eating on a regular schedule, but some children do better eating small amounts of food throughout the day. You and your toddler may feel better about her eating if you allow her to do what feels natural. If your child is a snacker, make healthy snacks available. One family set aside a kitchen drawer for their little snacker. Whenever Patrick felt hungry, he could go to "Patrick's drawer" and eat anything he found there. Patrick's mother kept the drawer stocked with crackers, pretzels, apples, and an occasional cookie or treat. Patrick loved to see what turned up each day in his drawer, and his mother enjoyed not arguing about meals. As long as your child is gaining weight and growing (well-child checkups are a must), he is probably doing just fine.

- *Learn to read the labels on foods.* There are a surprising number of hidden sugars and fats in the prepared foods young children love (breakfast cereals are a prime example), and too much sugar can wreak havoc with a child's appetite for nutritious food. Remember, balance is the key: your child needs a certain amount of fat to grow and be healthy, so the low-fat, low-sodium diet you may be following is not a good idea for her—nor is it necessary to substitute carrot sticks for holiday candies and treats. Don't be afraid to serve the same favorites over and over again; children aren't usually as fond of variety as their parents are. In fact, one way to get a suspicious eater to try new foods is to serve the "strange" item often. The food becomes familiar and children more willingly sample it. Your pediatrician can answer your questions about specific foods and help you feel confident that your child is healthy and growing.

- *Use mealtimes as an opportunity to teach.* While toddlers may resist force, they usually enjoy being invited to help Mom or Dad in the kitchen. Even young children can place napkins on the table, rinse lettuce for a salad, or place slices of cheese on hamburger buns. Children are almost always more competent and capable than adults think they are; we know two-year-olds who scramble eggs and stir together muffin recipes (with a parent's close supervision, of course).

  Teach children how to make their own peanut butter sandwiches or tortillas with cheese. Include them in the planning and preparation of meals, but let them know that in the future they can choose between eating what is on the table or making their own sandwiches or tortilla. Then, without making a fuss, sighing, or rolling your eyes, let them choose. If they complain about what is on the table, simply ask, "What can you do about that?"

  Inviting your child to help plan meals, choose ingredients at the grocery store ("Can you find the yellow bananas we need for your pudding?"), dish up servings, and help in the kitchen will not only take some of the struggle out of eating but will help you create a more resourceful, confident child.

- *Hang in there.* Most children change their eating habits over time, and the toddler who turns up his nose at veggies today may well love them next month. This miracle usually happens a great deal sooner if parents aren't shouting, lecturing, and pushing. Be patient; offer new foods occasionally, but don't insist. Enjoy mealtimes as an opportunity to gather your family together and share each other's company. In other words, relax a bit. This, too, shall pass!

Learning that you "can't make 'em do it" is a task that occupies most parents until their children are well into adolescence—and sometimes even beyond. Eventually, children will have to be able to manage their own eating habits. They will need to know what constitutes a healthy diet, how much to eat and at what time, and when to stop. Parents can allow their children to explore these concepts right from the beginning, acting as guides and teachers rather than enforcers. Mistakes, as we have said so often, are opportunities to learn—for parents and for children. Life with energetic young children will hold lots of challenges; mealtimes don't have to be among them.

12

Toileting

"It's My Job, Not Yours"

THE STRUGGLES PARENTS encounter with sleeping and eating pale in significance when we move to a discussion of toileting. No other topic in the world of raising young children arouses such strong emotions, it seems, as potty training.

The issue of toilet training has been blown out of proportion in our society. It can be the origin of feelings of guilt and shame, power struggles, revenge cycles, bids for undue attention, and competition between parents. Even if we didn't worry about it, our children would still become toilet trained in due time just because they would soon want to copy what everyone else does.

Paula Ascoli took a great deal of pride in the fact that her first child was using the toilet at the age of eighteen months. She was so pleased, in fact, that she thought about writing a book about toilet training to help other, less fortunate families. Before she could

> No other topic in the world of raising young children arouses such strong emotions, it seems, as potty training.

get around to it, however, her second child was born. Much to Paula's surprise, this child wanted nothing to do with her prize-winning toilet training techniques. In fact, despite being placed on the potty for long periods of time, this child was almost three years old before the "training" worked.

So much for genius. The reality is that children will use the toilet when they are ready to do so. You can cheer, beg, and threaten, but hang on to your diapers. Each child has his or her own unique schedule—and absolute control. What can parents do to set the stage for this important developmental milestone?

> The reality is that children will use the toilet when they are ready to do so. You can cheer, beg, and threaten, but hang on to your diapers. Each child has his or her own unique schedule—and absolute control.

Readiness

Q. *My son is going to be three next month, and he's still in diapers. Every time I change him, he kicks and moves a lot like he does not want me to change him. Does this mean I should start potty training him?*

A. Sounds like a great plan to us. Natural clues such as kicking and squirming can signal the decision to begin potty training. But squirming and resistance do not by themselves indicate a readiness for potty training. Your child's age is one factor you will want to consider.

There is no precise age at which children begin to use the potty. Few children master control before eighteen months, while most do so by age four. Complete nighttime success might take slightly longer and will still be within the typical developmental range. When children are truly ready, the process often takes only a few days or weeks. Physical readiness, emotional readiness, and environmental opportunities set children up for success.

Physical Readiness

Children give us a number of clues when they are physically ready to begin toilet training. Observe your child's behavior and ask yourself the following questions: Do long periods elapse between your child's diaper changes? Is her diaper dry after nap time? Does she stop what she is doing and get a look of concentration on her face when she wets herself? These things indicate increasing bladder capacity and awareness and mean that your child is becoming more able to connect her physical sensations with the need to use the toilet.

Children with regular bowel movements experience early success when their parents or caregivers tune in to those rhythms. However, this means adults may need more "training" than the child. Many parents know their child's patterns or facial clues and train themselves to put the child on the potty in time to catch the droppings in the toilet. This is one approach that helps a child become aware of her behavior and know what to do in response. After all, nothing succeeds like success.

Emotional Readiness

Q. *I have a son who needs to be potty trained. He turned three years old two months ago. He does not like to use the potty. He does not show me signs when he has to go, but he will tell me when to change him. Please, I need some advice!*

A. It does not take great intuition to recognize your desperation. It is hard to keep changing diapers as children grow older. Your son's reasons for not using the potty probably are magnified by your own discouragement. Take heart. He will succeed, but it may take more patience than you think you have. (Does it help to know that he probably won't still be wearing diapers when he goes to college?)

Here are some ideas to keep in mind:

- *Try to de-emphasize the whole issue.* Remember that when parents insist on a certain behavior, power struggles may ensue. Remaining calm and kind and refusing to argue over the toilet will ease the process for everyone concerned.

- *Sometimes a discussion of safety regarding the flushing toilet eases a child's mind.* Help him see that he is too big to fall through the toilet seat, allow him to flush the toilet to reassure himself that he is in control of this powerful, gulping monster, and reassure him that nothing scary will happen to him.

- *Don't become so focused on the bathroom that you lose your ability to enjoy the rest of your lives together.* Express your confidence in him; tell him that you know he will manage using the potty successfully one day. He, too, needs encouragement.

- *There are many ways to set the stage emotionally for successful potty training.* Young children often dislike having to lie still while being changed. Use this time to talk to your child, engaging her interest and thereby distracting her attention. Consider hanging a toy above the changing area, using a strip of elastic. Your child can swat, reach for, and handle the toy while she is being changed. This sort of distraction creates a more cooperative atmosphere, avoiding emotional resistance later on. Hang a musical mobile above the area or tape a fun picture on the ceiling. Changing these items occasionally sustains children's interest.

- *As your child matures, invite him to help with the job by handing you supplies, holding the clean diaper in readiness, or laying out the changing mat.* This increases opportunities to develop autonomy and sends the message that you believe your child is competent and capable. When he needs to be changed, show him ways he can help out. He can wash or wipe himself off, help empty the stool into the toilet bowl, and practice washing his own hands afterward. Inviting his participation also invites cooperation, an important ingredient for success. Changing older children while they stand up often invites more cooperation. Be sure to change a standing child on the floor or perhaps over the bed, so there is less danger of falling.

- *Lighten up and make toilet training fun.* One parent emptied the toilet bowl and painted a target in the bowl. His son could hardly wait to try to hit the bull's eye.

- *Avoid rewards and praise like stars on a chart or candy treats.* Instead, use encouraging statements and lots of hugs. Rewards can become more important to your child than learning socially appropriate behavior.

As with most skills, there will be accidents or mistakes during the process of mastering bladder and bowel control. Treating toilet accidents calmly and respectfully makes it less likely that power struggles, resistance, and lack of cooperation will result. Don't humiliate or shame your child when he has an accident; don't put him back in diapers. Simply help him clean up. Say, "It's okay. You can keep trying. I know you'll get it soon." With time and patience the skill will be mastered. (The section on toilet training in *Positive Discipline A–Z* by Jane Nelsen, Lynn Lott, and H. Stephen Glenn offers additional suggestions.)

Environmental Opportunities

Some of today's diapers make it difficult for children to respond to their own natural clues. Disposable diapers might do such a good job

As with most skills, there will be accidents or mistakes during the process of mastering bladder and bowel control. Treating toilet accidents calmly and respectfully makes it less likely that power struggles, resistance, and lack of cooperation will result.

of absorbing moisture that children do not notice when they are wet. Give children opportunities to notice what happens when they "go."

Allowing a child to go diaperless in the backyard on a warm day often provides an eye-opening experience. You can almost read her mind: "Wow! Look what I can do." The awareness of what happens physically often leads to mastery. One family found that their son became potty trained during the week of their family's camping vacation. Urinating in the woods with his older brother beat diapers any day!

Make the process easy. Moving to training pants or pull-ups eases the transition from diapers. Small potty seats or conversion rings for adult toilets with a small stool for climbing make perfect modifications. Be sure the child is wearing clothing that helps rather than hinders; elastic waistbands and loose articles are easier for small fingers to manage than snaps, buttons, and bows. The easier the on-and-off process, the more successful your little one will be.

Again, a parent's patient confidence makes a difference. Take young Andrew, for instance.

By the age of three or so, Andrew was ready to give up his diapers. Because he'd decided it was time, his mom and dad found the process delightfully easy: in just one day and two nights, Andrew was completely trained and accident-free.

Imagine, then, how surprised Andrew's mom and dad were when he demanded his diapers back after just one week. In checking out their son's request, his parents learned that Andrew had observed an interesting fact. Going to the bathroom, undoing his clothes, sitting down, cleaning up, and dressing again took more time away from important play than he was willing to spend. Andrew had discovered that diapers were simply less time-consuming, and he wanted to go back to them. When Andrew found that his parents weren't going to give in, however, he sighed—and remained in his "big boy pants," entering the grown-up world of bladder-regulated inconvenience.

If your little one wants to change his mind after the training process has been completed and celebrated, don't despair. Remain kind and firm, and the situation will undoubtedly resolve itself. And remember, each child will master toilet training but only on his *own* timetable.

If your little one wants to change his mind after the training process has been completed and celebrated, don't despair. Remain kind and firm, and the situation will undoubtedly resolve itself.

PART FIVE

Getting Along in the Great Big World

Discipline and Life Skills

Time passes, and children grow. Eventually—sooner for some than for others—your child will enter the world around him. He will need to know how to get along with others, to communicate, and to choose behaviors that help, not hinder, his progress in life.

Children have a great deal to learn in the first three years of life. They must master language and learn to recognize and cope with their own emotions and those of others. They must learn to match their behavior to their situation. And they must begin to believe in themselves, to have the courage to venture out into the world at large.

Parents usually have questions about these subjects—lots of them. Most parents find their toddler's behavior frustrating, irritating, and downright defeating at times. Most parents also wonder what they can do to help their children get along with others, live peacefully in their families, and succeed in life.

In the next few chapters we will examine how children relate to others. Learning to get along is a process that takes time, and parents and caregivers can smooth the way. We'll see how children learn to communicate, and we'll find ways to help them develop a sense of self-esteem. We'll also take a close look at discipline; we'll learn what doesn't work and what does. We will add effective Positive Discipline skills to the understanding you have gained of your unique child. The result will be a relationship you and your child can build on for the rest of your lives together.

13

Social Skills in the First Three Years

Did you know that a crying baby is practicing social skills? In the first months of a baby's life, crying brings adults, who provide food, comfort, and entertainment. By four months of age or so, the baby's social repertoire expands—he smiles at the adults who surround him. By five to eight months of age, the baby is giggling, cooing, and otherwise enchanting his grown-up companions.

Still, children don't truly discover that the world holds people other than themselves until they are between fourteen and twenty-four months of age. When a baby looks into a mirror, she sees an unknown being. It is well into the first year of life before a baby even recognizes the person in the mirror as herself! Knowing this can help adults comprehend how primitive her social interactions will be for a while. When adults understand that social skills don't develop naturally but must be taught, they may be less dismayed that children often hit, bite, push, and fight as they discover how to get along with others.

Social skills like sharing and playing develop through training, practice, and mistakes—especially mistakes. The road is not smooth;

When adults understand that social skills don't develop naturally but must be taught, they may be less dismayed that children often hit, bite, push, and fight as they discover how to get along with others.

emotional bumps and scrapes mark the landscape of early social experience, with an occasional real bite and scratch thrown in along the way. A knowledge of how social skills develop in young children will help parents and teachers provide both training and understanding as children learn to interact with their equally inexperienced peers.

Sharing

SHARING IS A big issue in the world of young children. We expect little people to take turns, to be happy with equal portions, to give up playing with a favorite toy. But children under the age of two are egocentric; that is, they are the center of their own world and everything else exists only as it relates to the center (which is, to be exact, "me"). This is not selfishness—it's natural human development.

"Mine"

MARY ROTH WAS *the first to raise her hand during the question-and-answer session at her parenting group. "My little girl, Jetta, is eighteen months old. I'm trying to teach her that everything does not belong to her," Mary said with an exasperated sigh. "She grabs my purse and says, 'Mine purse.' I try to reason with her and tell her, 'No, this is Mommy's purse,' but she just hangs on, repeating, 'Mine purse.' She does the same thing with the dog, the cereal box, and even the telephone."*

Guess what? As Mary will learn from her parenting leader, in Jetta's world everything is "mine." Jetta looks out at the world from its hub: herself. If you believe that the world begins and ends with you (and toddlers believe exactly that), it follows that everything in the world belongs to—you. No amount of logic will change Jetta's perspective, because it is simply the way she sees her place on the planet right now.

During the "mine" stage of development, do not waste energy on debates. Try saying, "You like Mommy's purse. Want to help me carry it?" Giving her accurate information, offering her a way to make her own small contribution to help you, and allowing her view of the world to persist until her development moves it forward makes far more sense than holding endless arguments over ownership. If you try to correct her thinking, you will almost certainly create a power struggle, perhaps setting a pattern for the future. Cooperation promises a much healthier future for both of you.

An inability to share does not portend a lifetime of selfishness. Possessiveness and ownership are normal steps before the ability to share gradually begins around the ages of three or four. Meanwhile:

- *Don't force your toddler to share.* Since the concept of sharing is meaningless to a toddler, you will not be accomplishing your goal and you may delay the ability in your child to share.

- *Begin teaching the process of sharing without expecting your child to understand.* Kindly and firmly remove an item that belongs to someone else or that she can't have, without lecturing or shaming. Offer whatever comfort you can, but don't try to shield your child from experiencing disappointment. You might say, "It is hard to share. You really wanted that." Empathy eases the pain and paves the way to later acceptance of sharing.

- *Model sharing.* Give your child bites or half of a special treat. Offer to let him hold something that is yours. Play

> An inability to share does not portend a lifetime of selfishness. Possessiveness and ownership are normal steps before the ability to share gradually begins around the ages of three or four.

trading games with him. "What do you want to share with me while I share this with you?"

- *Support your child's need to possess.* (Don't you have some possessions you don't want to share?) Help older children find another toy to play with, or provide more than one of the same toy.

Parallel Play

WHEN TODDLERS PLAY together, most of their play is "parallel play." They play near other children rather than with them. Jeffrey, for instance, is sixteen months old. When he takes his bath, it is Dad who splashes and floats the rubber duckie to him. It is Grandma who rocks him to sleep. At the child care center, the caregivers feed him, carry him, comfort him, and change him. There are other children present, but they are more like mysterious new toys. Jeffrey has begun to be curious about them and to explore them; he knows they cry when he pokes them, and when he tried to put one child's hair in his mouth it created quite a commotion. For now, Jeffrey is content to do his own thing while other children do theirs—at least, most of the time.

Sharing requires two participants. When one (or both) of those participants is the center of the universe, trouble is bound to result. Parents and teachers can help toddlers learn to share by taking time for training. They can demonstrate sharing and give it a name. They can encourage any moves in the direction of sharing. And they can understand that the process takes time, so they must have patience and allow for mistakes along the way.

It helps to remember that training at this stage is mostly preparatory; toddlers aren't quite developmentally ready to really share. Simply redirecting a toddler's attention can effectively defuse a combustible situation. The mistake many parents make is believing their toddlers can learn to share now. Training can start while they are toddlers, but they won't learn to share consistently, with an understanding of what sharing means, until much later (we know some adults who still haven't learned to share!). Adults may have difficulty sharing because of selfishness, but toddlers have difficulty sharing because they are toddlers. The best course of action is to begin a training program that is kind and firm, avoiding scolding and labels.

Sharing in the Real World of Toddlers

WHEN TWENTY-MONTH-OLD Susie grabs another child's toy, an adult can step in, remove the toy gently from Susie, return it to the other child, and carry Susie away to find some other interesting object to play with. Saying, "Tommy is playing with that toy right now" or "Let's find a toy that Susie enjoys" is all that is needed.

When Susie is two-and-a half and begins to attend a preschool, things change a bit. Susie is moving from a world where everything is "mine" to recognizing that the world contains other people. She no longer merely plays next to her companions but enjoys running around the playground with them. When Susie grabs a toy now, adults can respond differently than they did earlier. Susie is ready to learn and practice the social skill of sharing. A more appropriate response now is to take the toy and explore with her ways of learning to share with another child.

Susie and Tommy are playing in the block area when Susie grabs the toy car that Tommy has just picked up. Both children begin to yell, "It's mine! Give it to me!" Naturally, the uproar draws the attention of Mrs. McGee, the children's teacher. She walks over and gently takes the car.

"Susie," she asks, "do you want to play with this car?" "I want it," Susie agrees firmly. Mrs. McGee turns to Tommy. "Are you playing with the car, Tommy?" Tommy's lower lip juts out a bit as he says, "It's mine."

Mrs. McGee places the car in Tommy's hands and turns to Susie. "Susie, what do you think you could say to Tommy if you want to play with the car?" "I want to play with it?" Susie offers (with only a little sulk in her voice). Mrs. McGee agrees that's one way to ask. She suggests that Susie could also try saying, "May I play with the car?"

Tommy has been watching this exchange with interest. When his teacher asks him what he might say to Susie when she asks for the car, he responds right away. "Here, you can have it," he replies, handing the car to Susie. Mrs. McGee smiles. "It's nice of you to share, Tommy. What might you say if you weren't finished with the car?"

This is a new thought for Tommy. The teacher has made it clear that just asking may not be enough. She is helping Tommy learn that he has some options and can assert his own needs, but Tommy is momentarily baffled.

Mrs. McGee turns to Susie. "Can you think of something Tommy can say, Susie?" Susie has just the answer. "He could say, 'In a minute.'" Mrs. McGee nods. "That's a good idea. Perhaps he could say that he will give it to you in ten minutes. Would that work, Tommy?" Tommy nods, and Mrs. McGee encourages him to practice saying "I'm not done yet" to Susie.

Throughout this conversation, both children were invited to explore the possibilities available to them. Sharing is a skill that must be taught and practiced (even by adults). How will a child know what to do if no demonstrations are given? Remember, this is a period of intense language development. Providing the necessary words and ways to use them is part of the training process. Teaching and encouraging young children to "use their words" is a wonderful way to nurture social skills. However, it is important to remember that training is a process that must be repeated over and over as the developmental clock keeps ticking. It is the adults' job to guide continuously—not to expect that children should learn and remember after one experience, or a hundred. Many toddlers who had difficulty learning to

SUCCESSFUL STRATEGIES FOR TEACHING TODDLERS TO SHARE

There are many ways to take time for training in sharing.

- Model sharing yourself by saying, "I want to share my cake with you" or "Let's take turns bouncing the ball. I'll count to ten while you bounce it, then we'll count to ten while I bounce it."
- Give opportunities for sharing by saying, "I know that's your favorite toy. Which of your toys would you be willing to share with Michael for a while?"
- Acknowledge children's feelings. When children have difficulty sharing, acknowledge their feelings by saying, "I know it can be difficult to share. Sometimes I don't like to, either. You don't have to share all the time. I have faith that you will share when you are ready."
- Avoid passing judgment by shaming a child, labeling her as "naughty," or forcing a reluctant apology. Doing so does not encourage sharing.

share have grown up to become caring and giving people—especially if they grew up in a caring and giving environment.

Playing "Let's Pretend" with dolls or puppets is another way sharing can be modeled and practiced. Adults can act out a conflict between two children, showing what happened as well as other, more appropriate responses. Then children can practice, holding the puppets and exploring both the inappropriate and appropriate behavior. This invites children to recognize inappropriate behavior in others and, eventually, to notice and take responsibility for their own.

Hitting and Aggression

TODDLERS ARE SHORT on both language and social skills, and when they play together they can easily become frustrated. When they lack the ability to express what's wrong in words, hitting and other types of aggression sometimes result.

When you set one toddler down to "play" with another, neither is particularly sure of what the other is all about. Watch them eyeing one another and you can guess what they might be thinking. "What is this creature? Does it break? Can I taste it? What happens when I pull its hair or examine its eyelashes?" Walking up and hitting another child may be just a primitive form of saying hello.

Still, children under the age of two need to learn that pulling hair, poking eyes, and hitting are actions that hurt people and cannot be allowed. Firmness, coupled with removing the child temporarily and redirecting his attention to something else, works best. It does not help to scold or punish. How might we feel if someone scolded and punished us if we practiced a foreign language for a month but failed to speak it fluently? Social skills are a language that

HITTING

Q. Our fifteen-month-old son has started hitting my husband and me. He hits us on our backs or our heads if we're lying on the floor or on our face and heads if we're holding him. We thought this behavior might be an extension of his playing with the dog. We are trying to teach him how to pet the dog gently, but he hasn't quite grasped the idea. Instead, he hits the dog like he hits us. Is this something for us to worry about or does he just need to learn how to be gentle with dogs and people? Is he too young to understand the difference between hitting and affectionate patting? At any rate, how do we handle it? With the dog, we just take his

must be practiced, integrated, and learned at deeper levels when children are developmentally ready.

Little "Munch"kins— What to Do About Biting

ONE TYPE OF toddler aggression really sets off alarms for parents and for caregivers, and that is biting. Most biting incidents happen from about fourteen months to three years of age, which coincides with the development of spoken language. Biting may happen for a number of reasons. It may indicate frustration or anger, especially when a child isn't able to make herself understood with words. Some researchers believe that biting may be an angry variation of a kiss, while others think children bite out of curiosity or to observe their victim's (and the adults') reactions. Biting may even be the result of a vivid imagination. Twenty-month-old Teddy spent two weeks biting the ankle of anyone who wandered by before an observant adult realized he was playing the part of Shere Khan from *The Jungle Book.*

hand and help him pat gently while explaining about being gentle. When he hits us, we don't know what to do. Holding his hand just makes him mad and once we let go he does it again. If we put him down he cries. We have not had any problems with him until now. Should we be worried about it?

A. You are handling the situation with the dog well by teaching your son how to pat gently. Yes, he is too young to understand but not too young to start learning. Have patience as you keep teaching and providing practice. When he hits you, try putting him down and leaving the room immediately without saying a word. At this age, he will understand actions better than words.

Regardless of the reasons it happens, biting is very disturbing (not to mention painful) for the biter, the person who was bitten, and all adults involved.

Biting that occurs because a child lacks the words to express feelings and frustrations will diminish as he learns the verbal skills to express himself in more appropriate ways. Helping your child to express feelings verbally, providing carrot sticks to chew when frustration threatens, or holding a child's chin gently when he appears ready to bite may help resolve the problem. And no, biting the child back, washing out the mouth with soap, or placing Tabasco sauce on the tongue doesn't help; such responses are far more likely to escalate conflict than resolve it and may become abusive.

There are no magic remedies for biting. The most helpful responses begin with one essential element: supervision. Children who bite must be watched carefully. Can you detect a pattern in the biting? Does your child bite at a certain time of day, perhaps when she is hungry or tired or when too much is going on around her? If you spot a pattern, use your knowledge to be especially watchful during those times.

> There are no magic remedies for biting. The most helpful responses begin with one essential element: supervision.

Despite the most diligent supervision, biting often continues. Here are some things to do after a biting incident in which one child bites another:

Respond Quickly

Separate the children and check the seriousness of the injury. Your actions should be firm and decisive, but kind. Try to remain calm, not letting your own frustration or feelings of anger fuel your response. When we understand the developmental nature of biting, realize that time usually solves the problem, and know that we are doing all we can to deal with it, it becomes easier to manage this troubling behavior. Keep words to a minimum, such as a calm "No biting."

> ## What should you do if a child bites someone?
>
> - Respond quickly.
> - Involve both children in tending the wound.
> - Offer encouragement to both children.

Involve Both Children in Tending the Wound

Biting is particularly worrisome to parents because of the possibility of blood-borne disease. Adults and children tending the wound should wear plastic gloves, which provide protection and teach everyone concerned to avoid contact with blood. The child most at risk is the biter, who may have ingested blood, rather than the child who was bitten (this information—along with generous helpings of compassion and calm—may be useful when dealing with the bitten child's distraught family).

Offer Encouragement to Both Children

Both children, the child who did the biting and the bitten child, feel hurt and discouraged. Both need encouragement. No, we don't mean encouragement for the biter to bite again, but encouragement that you still care about them. Emotions run so high after a biting incident that the child who bites often finds himself villainized. Teachers march them to time-out and tell him to stay there all morning. Parents yell, send him to his room, and shun him. Parents frequently demand that preschools expel children who bite. It may be difficult in all the tumult to remember that this tiny person probably bit out of frustration, not evil intent. He cannot manage his impulses and probably can barely speak. What he really needs is a hug—and continued supervision. The child who was bitten suffers hurt feelings as well as hurt skin. It might help to ask the biter to help you comfort the child who was bitten. This provides healing for both children.

A bite happens in a nanosecond. Even a child holding his mother's hand might manage to chomp down on the child in the next stroller before his mom can stop him. In cases where biting becomes unmanageable, reducing time spent with other children may be necessary. Giving a youngster time to develop communication skills provides a needed break for everyone. If a child must be in continued contact with others, as in a child care setting, try having him carry a "bite-able" object. A small rubber teething ring pinned to his shirt with a diaper pin offers a temporary solution. Keep a close watch on the child while helping him learn he can always bite on his ring but he may not bite a person.

If a child continues to bite after the age of three, it may be helpful to get a speech and hearing evaluation to ensure that language skills are developing appropriately.

Social Interest

ALFRED ADLER DESCRIBED "social interest" as a real concern for others and a sincere desire to make a contribution to society. In addition to learning and perfecting the skills needed in social relationships, children learn about themselves and others through the social context of their experiences. As children enter into the lives of their families and schools, they want very much to feel that they belong. One of the most powerful ways to achieve a sense of belonging is to make a meaningful contribution to the well-being of others in the family or group. When elderly people continue to feel needed, it can add years to their lives. From cradle to grave, belonging and significance are among our most basic human needs. In the family or preschool, a wonderful way to encourage social interest is by sharing chores or the work the family does together.

For young children, there really is no difference between play and work. When a baby strives over and over again to grab a toy that is just out of reach, we say she is "playing," but actually she is hard at work, growing and developing new skills. Young children are usually eager to participate in whatever they see us doing, and the time to invite children to participate in the family is when they want to—not when they can do a task perfectly. Once you begin to see your youngster as an asset, he won't seem to be "underfoot" so much.

What Can My Little One Do?

FEELING CAPABLE AND able to contribute to others is so important. An eight-month-old hands her clean diaper to her dad when he is ready for it. A fifteen-month-old helps pile the bath toys into the tub. A two-year-old energetically helps mop up spills in the kitchen. These tasks are fun to youngsters and form the basic patterns for future learning. More critically, they plant the seeds for healthy self-esteem and allow children to feel a sense of belonging. Having a sense of belonging helps children feel encouraged, cooperative, and good about who they are, while not having a sense of belonging or feeling significant leads to discouragement—and, all too often, misbehavior, especially as children grow older.

Children, even little ones, can do any number of things to contribute to their family's well-being. As we watch our little ones during these first years of life, we must remember that they are watching us as well, and our examples speak more clearly than our words. Wise parents and care-givers will use a child's natural desire to imitate adult behavior to teach skills and to let children know their involvement and help are welcome.

When we consider the idea of social interest, our example again speaks loudest. We tell our children to treat animals gently; they watch us

> As we watch our little ones during these first years of life, we must remember that they are watching us as well, and our examples speak more clearly than our words.

angrily toss the cat outside after it claws the furniture. We want youngsters to learn compassion for others; they watch us sit comfortably on the bus while an elderly passenger stands nearby. We want them to be polite and quiet. They watch us holler across the room, admonishing squabbling youngsters, to "Quit yelling!" Which lesson will children remember? Our words or our actions?

A child watches an adult break off a piece of sandwich to offer to the birds hopping nearby, and he learns what sharing looks like. A child joins in a visit to a relative in a nursing home and learns to treasure human life. A child carries a fistful of flowers to present to a friend in the hospital and learns compassion. What lessons do you want to teach? Children are watching—and learning.

Working alongside your child can give both of you a great deal of pleasure as well as countless opportunities to learn. Helping your child feel competent, resourceful, and confident will help him succeed at home, in his relationships in the outside world, and in the challenges life brings to all of us.

14

Discipline in the First Three Years

Some of the information in this book was originally included in our book *Positive Discipline for Preschoolers.* Even though that book included chapters on the first three years of life, our publishers were reluctant to highlight that fact in the title because of their concern that people might think we were advocating "punishment" for babies.

We hope that by now you understand that we do not advocate punishment of any kind. When people talk about "discipline" they often mean "punishment," usually because they believe the two are one and the same. Real discipline, however, involves teaching; in fact, the word itself comes from the Latin root *disciplina,* which means "to teach." Interestingly enough, it is the same root from which we get the word "disciple." As you may have noticed, Positive Discipline is about teaching, understanding, encouraging, and communicating—not about punishing.

Most of us absorbed our ideas about discipline from our own parents, our society, and years of tradition and assumptions. We often believe that children must suffer (at least a little) or they won't learn anything. But many things have changed in the past few decades. Our society and culture have changed rapidly, our understanding of how children grow and learn has changed, and consequently the ways we teach children to be capable, responsible, confident people must change as well. Punishment may seem to work in the short term. But over time, we know that it creates rebellion, resistance, or children who just don't believe in their own worth. There is a better way, and this book is devoted to helping parents discover it.

Why Some Parents Don't Accept Nonpunitive Methods

BECAUSE ALL CHILDREN (and all parents) are unique individuals, there are usually several nonpunitive solutions to any problem. Some parents we met at lectures and parenting classes didn't seem to understand or accept these solutions, and it took awhile to realize that it takes a dramatic shift in thinking before some parents can be open to nonpunitive suggestions. Parents who can't absorb the idea of nonpunitive discipline often are asking the wrong questions. They usually want to know:

- How do I make my child mind?
- How do I make my child understand "no"?
- How do I get my child to listen to me?
- How do I make this problem go away?

Most frazzled parents want answers to these questions at one time or another, but they are based on short-term thinking. Parents will be eager for nonpunitive alternatives when they ask the right questions—and see the results this change in approach creates for them and their children:

- How do I help my child feel capable?

- How do I help my child feel belonging and significance?

- How do I help my child learn respect, cooperation, and problem-solving skills?

- How do I get into my child's world and understand his developmental process?

- How can I use problems as opportunities for learning—for my child and for me?

These questions address the big picture and are based on long-term thinking. We have found that when parents find answers to the long-term questions, the short-term questions take care of themselves: children do "mind" and cooperate (at least, most of the time), they understand "no" when they are developmentally ready (and are involved in solutions to problems), and they listen because parents listen to them and talk in ways that invite listening. Problems are solved more easily when children are involved in the process.

We have included discipline tips in every chapter of this book (keeping in mind that discipline has nothing to do with punishment). In this chapter, we will look at why punishments should be avoided, and we will present a summary of the many non-punitive methods that will help your child develop into a capable and loving person.

Discipline Methods to Avoid

IF YOU ARE screaming, yelling, or lecturing, stop. If you are spanking, stop. If you are trying to gain compliance through threats, warnings, and lectures, stop. All of these methods are disrespectful and encourage doubt, shame, and guilt—now, and in the future. Ultimately, punishment creates more misbehavior.

"Wait just one minute," you may be thinking. "These methods worked for my parents. You're taking away every tool I have to manage my child's behavior. What am I supposed to do, let my children do anything they want?" No. We are not advocating permissiveness. Permissiveness is disrespectful and does not teach important life skills. True discipline guides, teaches, and invites healthy choices. As we've discovered, we can never really control anyone's behavior but our own, and our attempts to control our children usually create more problems, more power struggles, and more of what we've been trying to control! Later in this chapter, we offer several methods that invite cooperation (when applied with a kind and firm attitude) while encouraging your toddler to develop a healthy sense of autonomy and initiative.

Life with an active, challenging toddler becomes much easier when we accept that positive learning does not take place in a threatening atmosphere. Children don't listen when they are busy feeling scared, hurt, or angry. When children feel threatened, they

SHE WANTS WHAT SHE WANTS

Q. My sixteen-month-old girl does whatever she wants even though my husband and I have tried various methods of punishment. We've tried saying no, putting her in time-out, slapping her hands, and yelling, but nothing seems to work on her. She throws some pretty bad temper tantrums, too. I feel like we have tried everything. I am opposed to spanking and have given into hand slapping as a compromise, but it doesn't work either. My husband thinks we should spank so she knows she has done something wrong and will not repeat it. What do you suggest?

A. You are experiencing the frustration of so many parents who do not understand their child's development. Punishment—no matter what sort we use—is likely to produce what we call the Four R's of Punishment:

go into a defensive mode. Defensive behavior may look like compliance, rebellion, or anything in between, because the child needs to regain his precious sense of belonging and significance—and will do almost anything to get it. We need to know that our children are learning the right things, that they know they belong and have significance, and that they can trust us, learn from us, and let us know what their world feels like. Punishment derails the learning process. Kind and firm discipline balances security and boundaries with the love and respect children need so much in their early years.

Time-Out: Positive Versus Punitive

MOST PARENTS USE something called a time-out, but few really understand what it is or how best to use it with young children. There

1. Resentment

2. Rebellion

3. Revenge

4. Retreat, through
   a. Sneakiness ("I just won't get caught next time") or
   b. Low self-esteem ("I really am a bad person")

Has any young child you know responded in these ways? The latest brain research suggests that punishment hampers optimal brain development, so it should come as no surprise that the punishments you've tried are not working. Take heart: you have not yet "tried everything." The rest of this chapter will help you understand why punishment is not effective and teach you what to do instead.

are several points that need to be made regarding positive time-out for children who have not yet reached the age of reason:

- *Time-outs should not be used with children under the age of two-and-a-half.* Until children reach the age of reason, which starts around age two-and-a-half (and is an ongoing process that even some adults have not fully mastered), supervision and distraction are the most effective parenting tools. This means simply that young children need constant supervision and removal, kindly and firmly, from what they can't do and guidance to an activity they can do. Most parents have at one time or another found themselves in a heated debate with someone who only comes up to their kneecap—and most will admit that reason, lecturing, and argument just don't work. Remember, young children often can read the energy of your feelings and understand that you want something; they may even be able to guess what that something is. But they do not understand the logic of your arguments in the way you think they do.

  Before the age of reason, children can't understand the reasoning behind punishment, either. How might a young child interpret a time-out? Typically, time-out is only punishment renamed. Punishment may stop the behavior for the moment, but what long-range messages have children received? They may be deciding, "I'm bad." "I'll get even and hurt back." "I'll hit others when I'm bigger." "Yelling at people is a good way to communicate." Or "I won't get caught next time." Children aren't consciously aware of the decisions they are making, but they are making decisions nonetheless.

- *Children do better when they feel better.* Even younger children can benefit from an opportunity to "cool off," especially if you go with them. We know of one mother who used "positive time-out" successfully with her eighteen-month-old child. That it "worked" was undoubtedly due to her attitude. She would say to her child, "Would you like to lay on your comfy pillow for a while?" Sometimes he would just toddle off to his pillow and lie down until he felt better. If he hesitated, she would ask, "Do you want me to go with you?"

- *Your attitude is the key.* Time-out should not be used as a punishment, but as a way to help children understand their feelings, calm down, and choose better behavior. The procedure for setting up "positive time-out" for children over age two-and-a-half is explained thoroughly in *Positive Discipline for Preschoolers* (and in most of our other books as well). A brief explanation is that the most useful sort of time-out is one that is intended to help a child understand and master her feelings—a cooling-off time rather than a time to "think about how bad you've been."

    If you decide to try this sort of time-out with your little one, create a safe, comfortable area where she enjoys spending time. Remember, you're not punishing her; you're helping her to feel better so she can make better choices about her behavior. Pillows, stuffed animals, or favorite soothing toys will help. Before the age of two-and-a-half, you might find it helpful to go to time-out with your child. Say, "Let's take some time out to read a book or listen to music until we feel better." If you feel out of control, let your own behavior show your child how to use time out by going to your room, taking some deep breaths, or sitting by yourself until you calm down.

Time-out should not be used as a punishment, but as a way to help children understand their feelings, calm down, and choose better behavior.

- *No parenting tool works all of the time.* Be sure to have more than just time-out in your toolbox. It is important to have many different parenting skills and tools. There is never one tool—or three, or even ten—that is effective for every situation and for every child. Filling your parenting toolbox with healthy, nonpunitive alternatives will help you avoid the temptation to punish when your child challenges you—and he undoubtedly will! The more you know, the more confident you will feel as you cope with the ups and downs of life with a young child.

Georgia Popolos sighed in exasperation—this was Amanda's third tantrum this afternoon. Two-year-old Amanda was having a rough day; Luke, her older brother, had invited a houseful of friends over to play for the afternoon and Amanda hadn't been able to take her usual nap. Now, cranky and miserable, she had ripped half the pages from Georgia's new magazine then swept it off the table. She gazed up at her mom with stubborn defiance—and a trembling chin.

> Filling your parenting toolbox with healthy, nonpunitive alternatives will help you avoid the temptation to punish when your child challenges you—and he undoubtedly will!

Georgia was tired herself. She stifled the desire to lecture her small daughter and drew a deep breath. "Would you like to curl up in your special corner with your blankie?" she asked Amanda.

Amanda only shook her head and sat down in a heap amid the torn pages of the magazine.

"Well, how about playing with your dollhouse?" Georgia asked helpfully, reaching out to take Amanda's hand and lead her to her favorite toy.

Amanda yanked her hand away and let her little body go limp on the floor, shaking her head vehemently.

Georgia sighed again and sat down near her daughter. "Let's see," she thought, "what else did they suggest in that parenting class?"

Finally she rose and gave Amanda a weary smile. "You know what, honey?" she said as kindly as she could. "I need to start dinner—and I sure could use some help. You can lie here and rest or you can join me in the kitchen and help me wash the let-

tuce—it's up to you." And with that, Georgia walked into the kitchen.

For a few moments, the sniffling and kicking from the family room floor continued. Soon, however, a small, tear-streaked face peered around the kitchen corner. Amanda looked uncertainly at her mom, but Georgia just smiled and gestured toward the sink.

Encouraged, Amanda went to get her little stool, dragged it over to the sink, and began dunking lettuce leaves in the water. By the time Amanda's dad arrived home, harmony had been restored, the ripped magazine had been cleared away, and Georgia, Luke, and Amanda were working companionably together to set the table. Georgia was glad that positive time-out wasn't the only tool in her parenting toolbox.

It is often true that what works with young children one day will not work the next. But if you've taken the time to know your child and to learn all the different ways there are to teach and encourage, chances are good that you will find *something* that works—just for today.

• *Always remember your child's development and capabilities.* Understanding what is (and is not) age-appropriate behavior will help you not to expect things that are beyond the ability of your child.

The Stantons took their two-year-old twin boys to a band concert featuring their seven-year-old as a flute soloist. The twins were fascinated with the concert—for about ten minutes. Then they found other ways to entertain themselves. One twin started crawling under the seats, and the other soon joined the fun. Mr. Stanton took the twins outside and spanked them for not sitting still. The twins cried loudly and could not be taken back inside for the rest of the concert. Mr. Stanton was very disappointed that he missed his daughter's solo, his daughter was disappointed that her father didn't hear her, and Mrs. Stanton and the twins were upset about the spanking. Everyone was miserable.

It is a sad thing when children are punished for doing things that are developmentally appropriate, even though they are not situationally appropriate. It is unreasonable to expect two-year-olds to sit for long periods of time. However, it is not okay to allow children to disturb others. Since the Stantons didn't choose to leave their twins with a caregiver, it would have been more effective for them to take turns bringing their children outside so they could take turns hearing parts of the concert. It would not be appropriate to punish the children, but it would be appropriate to provide a distraction, such as reading them a story. This kind of "time-out" removes children from inappropriate expectations without making everyone miserable.

POINTS TO REMEMBER ABOUT POSITIVE TIME-OUT

- Time-out works best with children older than two-and-a-half.

- Children do better when they feel better. Even younger children may benefit from an opportunity to "cool off," especially if you go with them.

- Your attitude is the key. Time-out should not be used as a punishment, but as a way to help children understand their feelings, calm down, and choose better behavior.

- No parenting tool works all of the time. Be sure to have more than just time-out in your toolbox!

- Always remember your child's development and capabilities.

Guiding Versus Controlling

LIKE IT OR NOT, our attitude as parents determines whether or not we create a battleground or an environment where a child feels safe to explore, make mistakes, and grow within appropriate boundaries.

Lynn Fitzpatrick sometimes wondered why she had been so eager to have a child. It felt to her that both she and her little boy were out of control. He rarely chose to "mind" her, and she did not like the fact that she found herself yelling and using punitive methods. She especially did not like the fact that nothing seemed to work!

Lynn attended a parenting class for parents of preschoolers and learned about age-appropriate behavior. When she changed her expectations about the "perfect child" who would obey her every command, she began to enjoy her child's experimentation with autonomy and initiative. Instead of trying to control him, she started guiding him away from inappropriate behavior by showing him what he could do.

She was most amazed at how much her child seemed to calm down when Lynn calmed down. Frustrating episodes occurred less often and were solved more quickly because of her new understanding. When Lynn stopped focusing on making her child "mind," things between them finally began to work.

Methods That Invite Cooperation

SO THE STAGE is set. If punishment doesn't work, what does? Yes, we need to have several methods available—but what are they? Here are some suggestions. Remember that nothing works all the time for all children, and as your own special little one grows and changes,

TEN METHODS FOR IMPLEMENTING POSITIVE DISCIPLINE

1. Get children involved.
2. Teach respect by being respectful.
3. Use your sense of humor.
4. Get into your child's world.
5. If you say it, mean it, and if you mean it, follow through with kindness and firmness.
6. Create routines.
7. Offer choices.
8. Provide opportunities to help.
9. Be patient.
10. Provide lots of supervision, distraction, and redirection.

you'll have to return to the drawing board many times, but these ideas may form the foundation for years of effective parenting.

Get Children Involved

Instead of telling children what to do, find ways to involve them in decisions and to draw out what they think and perceive. "What" and "how" questions are one way to do this. Ask, "What do you think will happen if you push your tricycle over the curb?" or "How should we get ready for day care?" For preverbal children, say, "Next, we ____," while kindly and firmly showing them instead of telling them. Children given choices experience a healthy sense of personal power and autonomy.

Teach Respect by Being Respectful

Parents usually believe children should show respect, not have it shown to them. But children learn respect by seeing what it looks like in action. Be respectful when you make requests. Don't expect a child to do something "right now" when you are interrupting something she is thoroughly engaged in. Give her some warning. "We need to leave in a minute. Do you want to swing one more time or ride the teeter-totter?" Carry a small timer around with you. Teach her to set it to one or two minutes. Then let her put the timer in her pocket so she can be ready to go when the timer goes off.

Remember, too, that shame and humiliation are disrespectful and a child who is treated with disrespect is likely to return the favor. Kindness and firmness show respect for your child's dignity, your own dignity, and the needs of the situation.

Use Your Sense of Humor

No one ever said parenting had to be boring or unpleasant. Often, laughter is the best way to approach a situation. Try saying, "Here comes the tickle monster to get children who don't listen." Learn to laugh together and to create games to get unpleasant jobs done quickly. Humor is one of the best—and most enjoyable—parenting tools.

It is amazing how many children who resist a direct order will respond with enthusiasm when that order becomes an invitation to play. Try telling your toddler, "I bet you can pick up all your little cars before I count to ten," or "I wonder if you can brush your teeth and get into your pajamas before Dad does."

Get into Your Child's World

Be empathetic when your child cries (or has a temper tantrum) out of frustration with his lack of abilities. Empathy does not mean rescuing. It does mean understanding. Give your child a hug and say,

"You're really upset right now. I know you want to stay, but it's time to leave." Then hold your child and let him experience his feelings before you move on to the next activity.

Getting into your child's world also means seeing the world from his perspective and recognizing his abilities—and his limitations. Occasionally ask yourself how you might be feeling (and acting) if you were your child. It can be illuminating to view the world through a smaller person's eyes.

If You Say It, Mean It, and If You Mean It, Follow Through with Kindness and Firmness

Children usually sense when you mean what you say and when you don't. It's usually best not to say anything unless you mean it and can say it respectfully—and can follow through with dignity and respect. The fewer words you say, the better! Again, this means redirecting or showing a child what she can do instead of punishing her for what she can't do. This might mean wordlessly removing a child from the slide when it is time to go, rather than getting into an argument or a battle of wills. When this is done kindly, firmly, and without anger, it will be both respectful and effective.

> Children usually sense when you mean what you say and when you don't. It's usually best not to say anything unless you mean it and can say it respectfully—and can follow through with dignity and respect.

Create Routines

Routines can be created for every event that happens over and over: getting up, bedtime, dinner, shopping, and so on. As soon as your children are old enough, get them involved in helping you create routine charts. Then ask your child, "What do we need to do next on our routine chart?" For children who are younger, say, "Now it's time for us to _____." Be sure not to confuse these with sticker or reward charts. Routine charts simply list sequences of events, to act as guidelines for common tasks.

Offer Choices

Offering choices gives children a sense of power: They have the power to choose one possibility or another. Choices also invite a child to use his thinking skills as he contemplates what to do. And, of course, toddlers often love it when choices include an opportunity to help. "What is the first thing we should do when we get home—put the groceries away, or read a story?" "Would you like to carry the blanket or the cracker box as we walk to the car?" Be sure the choices are developmentally appropriate and are options with which you are comfortable.

Provide Opportunities to Help

Toddlers often resist a command to get in the car but respond cheerfully to a request like "Will you carry the keys to the car for me?" Activities that might easily have become power struggles and battles can become opportunities for laughter and closeness if we use our instincts and our creativity.

Be Patient

Understand that you may need to teach your child many things over and over before he is developmentally ready to understand. Don't take your child's behavior personally and think your child is mad at you, bad, or defiant. Remain the adult in the situation and do what needs to be done without guilt and shame.

Provide Lots of Supervision, Distraction, and Redirection

Minimize your words and maximize your actions. As Rudolf Dreikurs said, "Shut your mouth and act." Quietly take your child by the hand and lead her to where she needs to go. Show her what she can do instead of what she can't do. When you understand that children don't really understand "no" the way you think they should, it makes more sense to use distraction, redirection, or any of the respectful Positive Discipline methods.

Accept Your Child's Uniqueness

REMEMBER THAT CHILDREN develop differently and have different strengths. Expecting from a child what he cannot give will only frustrate both of you. Your sister's children may be able to sit quietly in a restaurant for hours, while yours get twitchy after just a few minutes no matter how diligently you prepare (refer to chapter 8 on temperament and chapter 9 on developmentally appropriate behavior for more on this subject). That being the case, you may decide to save that fancy meal out for a time when you can enjoy it in adult company—or for when your children have matured enough for all of you to enjoy it together.

It may help to think of yourself as a coach, helping your child succeed and learn how to do things. You're also an observer, learning who your child is as a unique human being. Never underestimate the ability of a young child. Watch carefully as you introduce new opportunities and activities; discover what your child is interested in, what your child can do by himself, and what he needs help learning from you.

A Word About "Multiples"

PRACTICING POSITIVE DISCIPLINE takes energy, thoughtfulness, and patience. For some parents, though, it may sound downright impossible. "What do I do," you may be wondering, "if I have more than one infant?"

These days multiple births are far more common than they once were. Treatment for infertility is widely available and often results in the birth of twins, triplets, quadruplets—even septuplets! Most parents, after they've done the inevitable math about the number of diapers and feedings they will need per day, begin to wonder, "If teaching, training, and encouraging one toddler is tough, is it even possible when there is more than one? How will I keep myself healthy? And what if, as is sometimes the case, my little ones are premature and have medical or developmental problems? How will I cope?"

> It may help to think of yourself as a coach, helping your child succeed and learn how to do things.

Sarah and Peter Anderson had all of these questions. They had two delightful daughters, a seven-year-old and a four-year-old, but they wanted to add a son to their family. Sarah and Peter decided to try one more time, but they could never have anticipated the surprise nature had in store for them.

Midway through Sarah's pregnancy her doctor delivered the news: Yes, they were going to have a son. They were also going to have two more daughters. Sarah was carrying triplets.

The first months of the babies' lives were chaotic for the family. The babies never seemed to eat or sleep at the same time, and even when Sarah and Peter took turns caring for them, the parents frequently went without sleep. The older girls were delighted with the babies and were usually a real help to their frazzled parents, but adjusting to being a family of seven felt completely overwhelming to all of them. Sarah and Peter's social life disappeared, and their finances were strained. One of the baby girls suffered from respiratory problems and required regular medical care. Sometimes the older girls sulked and whined about how much time and attention the triplets took up. But the fun didn't really begin until the babies became mobile.

As soon as they could scoot, the triplets embarked on the adventure of exploring their world. When one discovered how much fun it was to launch stuffed toys off the second-floor balcony, the other two had to try. Peter and Sarah didn't get to clean up just one batch of thrown cereal— they usually had to clean up three!

Peter walked into the bedroom one afternoon to find his wife sobbing miserably on the bed. "I love the babies so much," she sniffed, "but I'm so tired. I can't keep up with them, and they're getting out of control. I don't have time for the girls, and you and I haven't been out in months. I've looked for a child care center, but it's just too expensive for three babies. I don't know what to do!"

We want to stress that Positive Discipline skills do work for multiples—but it is also true that having more than one active toddler can try the patience of even the most devoted parent. Getting through the first three years of life is a bit easier if you keep the following suggestions in mind:

- *Ask for help.* Don't be shy about requesting assistance. You'll cope far better with the inevitable stress of raising multiples if you occasionally have time to be by yourself or alone with your partner. Many communities offer respite care, which are drop-in centers where trained volunteers will watch your little ones for an hour or two. Some child care centers may also be willing to give you a "group rate," especially if you offer to spend a little time there each week volunteering.

- *Look for support from other parents of multiples.* Because multiple births have become more frequent, your community may have a chapter of "Mothers of Multiples" or another support group. Such groups offer resources and invaluable help in the task of adjusting to life with more than one active toddler. Your doctor or hospital may be able to put you in touch with a local group. Resources also can be found on the Internet.

- *Choose your battles.* You're only human; you may have to decide where your limited energy can best be used. Sarah and Peter decided that they would kindly and firmly remove food when throwing began—but that they could live with stuffed animals cascading from the balcony.

- *Teach your children to help themselves—and each other.* Taking time for training and encouragement becomes even more important when you have multiples. Your little ones can learn to assist and support each other. If you provide opportunities for them to learn new skills, your task will eventually be much easier.

- *Beware of "scapegoating" one of your multiples.* It frequently seems that one toddler will instigate most of the activity. If one of your multiples seems to be the leader, work to use his or her influence to teach and cooperate— not to blame. Sibling fighting is probably inevitable, but putting children "in the same boat" and refusing to referee or take sides will help. Invite them to go to separate corners until they are ready to come out *not* fighting.

- *Recognize and encourage the uniqueness of each child.* It can be tempting to treat multiples as mirror images, not only dressing them alike but assuming they have the same temperaments and abilities. Take time to understand the ways in which your children differ. If possible, allow them to have separate space and individual possessions, and let them know you value them for the unique people they are. Respond, too, to the cues they give you about their own relationships with each other. Many multiples remain extraordinarily close for a lifetime.

Your multiples will undoubtedly attract a great deal of attention—and you will probably have moments when you wonder if you will survive. Be gentle with yourself; remember the value of kindness and firmness. Hang on to your sense of humor. And try to enjoy!

Hugs, Hugs, Hugs

IN OUR WORKSHOPS, we have an enlightening activity. We ask for twelve volunteers, six to play the role of children and six to be parents. We then ask them to team up as parent and child. We ask the "children" to leave the room while we give instructions to the "parents" in front of the other adults.

When the children return to the room, we ask them to role-play temper tantrums. The parents have been instructed to wait a few seconds and then go to their child and say, "I need a hug." If the child doesn't give a hug, the parent waits a few seconds and asks again. If there still is no response, the parent asks a third time, "I need a hug. Come find me when you are ready." Then the parent walks away.

It is so much fun to watch what happens. Usually more than half the children give their parents a hug on the first request. Most of the others give a hug on the second request. Humans being humans, there are always two or three who hang on to the power struggle. However, when their parents walk away, they look confused or shocked. Most of them hurry off to find their parents for a hug.

We ask the participants what they were thinking and feeling in each role. The adults who played the parents love the exercise because it gives them a plan that helps them unhook from their child's behavior. The adults playing the children share that they feel unconditionally loved and motivated to change their behavior—after the initial shock of getting a response so different from what they expected.

We'll say it again: since misbehaving children are discouraged children, the best way to help them stop misbehaving is to help them feel encouraged. Where did we ever get the crazy idea that in order to help children do better, we first have to make them feel worse? Children *do* better when they *feel* better. Asking for or giving a hug is just one possibility; your own wisdom, creativity, and love for your child will help you discover many more.

15

Building Healthy Self-Esteem Through Encouragement

Learning the fine art of encouragement is one of the most important skills of effective parenting. Experts who study human behavior and development tell us that a healthy sense of self-esteem is one of the greatest assets a child can have, and parents who know how to encourage, have faith, and teach have the best chance of helping their children develop self-esteem.

What exactly is self-esteem? Where does it come from? Self-esteem is, quite simply, the confidence and self-satisfaction each one of us has in ourselves. Self-esteem comes from feeling a sense of belonging, believing that we're capable, and knowing our contributions are valued and worthwhile.

Self-esteem gives children the courage to take risks in life and to welcome new experiences—everything from tackling the stairs with unsteady steps to being the first kid at day care to say hello each day to trying out for the football team or honors orchestra later in life.

Children who lack self-esteem fear failure and often don't believe in themselves even when they possess wonderful talents and abilities.

Self-esteem doesn't just happen in children; it evolves from their beliefs and experiences. We can't give them self-esteem—we have to help them develop it. But how?

> Self-esteem doesn't just happen in children; it evolves from their beliefs and experiences. We can't give them self-esteem—we have to help them develop it.

Mistakes Parents Make in the Name of Self-Esteem

PARENTS (AND TEACHERS) are usually well aware these days that children need a healthy sense of self-esteem. They may try their very best to nurture this quality in the children in their care. All too often, though, their best efforts backfire. Before we look at effective ways to build self-esteem, let's look at some methods that don't work.

Trying to Give Children Self-Esteem Through Excessive Praise and Pep Talks

Praise can actually be discouraging instead of encouraging. When parents constantly tell children, "You are such a good girl! I'm so proud of you!" children may become *approval junkies.* Instead of developing self-esteem, they may decide, "I'm okay only if someone thinks I am." They may feel pressure to be perfect to avoid disappointing their parents. Or they may give up because they believe they can't live up to the praise—and the high expectations that usually go along with it.

Overprotecting or Rescuing Children

Many parents are afraid their children will suffer forever if they have to deal with discomfort or disappointment. Overly protected chil-

INEFFECTIVE METHODS FOR BUILDING SELF-ESTEEM

- Trying to give children self-esteem through excessive praise and pep talks.
- Overprotecting or rescuing children.
- Wanting children to be "better" (or just different).

dren may decide, "I can't handle problems. I can't survive disappointment. I need others to take care of me and rescue me." Or they may decide that it's easier to let others take responsibility for them. Either way, overprotected children rarely develop the competence and self-confidence that might help them handle life's challenges as they grow.

Wanting Children to Be "Better" (or Just Different)

Since the primary goal of all children is to feel that they belong and are significant, it is devastating when they discover that their parents don't love them unconditionally. When the mother of Travis, an active, high-energy child, says, "Why can't you be as calm and well-behaved as Johnny?" Travis may decide, "I'm not good enough. It really doesn't matter what I do—my mom doesn't like me." This kind of discouragement is the foundation for most misbehavior. There is nothing as encouraging and effective as loving, unconditional acceptance. This does not mean that parents applaud their children's misbehavior and weaknesses; it does mean that parents realize that they help their children best when they accept them for who they are, with all their unique strengths and weaknesses—and practice kind, firm discipline, teaching, and encouragement to help them grow into capable, confident young people.

Kindness and Firmness

THIS BRINGS US back to a phrase we have repeated over and over: be kind and firm at the same time. Notice how this phrase fits as you look at the mistakes listed above. Teaching children that they are loved only when they behave in ways that are cute, sweet, or undemanding is not kind. Kindness shows unconditional love. Firmness provides guidance. Kindness and firmness at the same time provide children with many opportunities to develop self-esteem. Let's look now at what helps children develop healthy self-esteem.

Encouragement

Praise is cheap and, in this world of ours, is often mass-produced—and therefore meaningless. Little smiley faces that say "great kid" can be stamped on any child's hand. Real encouragement is more selective, however, noticing and validating the uniqueness of each individual.

Little Amy waited until her twelfth month to make her walking debut. Her family had traveled across the country to visit grandparents in Florida. One afternoon with her parents, grandparents, and siblings gathered around, Amy decided the time to display her skills had arrived. She grinned at her family, then relinquished her hold on the sofa and with heart-stopping wobbles took her first steps—straight into Grandma's eager arms. Her family was ecstatic. "You can do it!" they called, their faces wreathed in smiles. "That's it. Just take it slow. Just a little further. Go Amy! You've got it! Hooray!" Amy's grin almost split her face in two as she basked in her family's love. Now, that's encouragement!

The praise version might have sounded more like this: "Good girl! I'm so proud of you."

Many parents become confused about the difference between praise and encouragement, so let's take a closer look. In the scenes described above, the former encourages the task, while the latter praises the person. Many children, when praised, form the belief that they are "good" only if they accomplish a task. Praise usually requires a completed task, while encouragement speaks to the effort. In other words, praise is often conditional, while encouragement is unconditional.

An important clue that will help you understand the difference between praise and encouragement is to get into your child's world. Notice if your child is depending too much on the opinion of others—a dangerous result of praise. On the other hand, little ones love an audience and often enthusiastically invite you to "Watch me! Watch me!" So, don't become paranoid about the difference between praise and encouragement. Just be aware of the possible perceptions of your child. Do your statements convey conditional or unconditional love and support?

Showing Faith

Amy's family offered her encouragement most effectively by allowing her to experiment with the process of walking—and by not intervening unnecessarily. Amy's family might have chosen to rescue their fragile baby. Grandma might have called out, "Be careful. Quick, someone, catch the baby." Mom or Dad might have swooped in to hold Amy's hand, block her path, or pick her up. Older brother might have grabbed Amy from behind to steady her.

There was a risk that Amy might fall, but Amy's family gave her the chance to take that risk. Risks imply the possibility of failure, but without risk there can never be success. Amy took a risk and managed her first steps. No praise could replace her feeling of accomplishment in that moment. Self-esteem is that experience of "I can do it!" We build self-esteem in our children when we balance our need to protect them with their need to take risks, tackle new challenges, and explore their capabilities.

Balance, however, is essential. Imagine a parent believing that her child should never be discouraged from exploring his environment.

She feels that limiting his activities might result in frustrating his curiosity. So when little Michael heads into the street, she runs to the intersection and flags the cars to a stop, allowing Michael to stroll contentedly among the fenders. This is not encouragement. What Michael needs is supervision and lots of teaching about the danger of intersections, lest he decide to try crossing the street when his mother isn't there to play traffic cop.

Encouragement does not mean remaking the world to fit your toddler's every whim. Kindly and firmly removing a child from the street does limit his exploring; it also protects him from danger and does not allow him to believe wandering in the street is safe. Wise parents weigh their children's choices and environments to determine which experiences offer opportunities for growth and which are simply too dangerous. Allowing a child to take reasonable risks and learn new skills is encouragement. Facing challenges and experiencing success builds self-esteem.

> Wise parents weigh their children's choices and environments to determine which experiences offer opportunities for growth and which are simply too dangerous. Allowing a child to take reasonable risks and learn new skills is encouragement.

Loving the Child You Have

Most of us have dreams of who our child will be. We may hope for a child who is quiet and dreamy, one who is energetic and outgoing, or one who possesses some other combination of qualities and talents. We may even want a child exactly like ourselves (parents and children do not necessarily come in matched pairs!).

Janice Chandra had dreamed of her child's babyhood. She had been delighted to have a little girl, and she had painstakingly furnished the nursery in pastel-colored lace and ruffles. She bought ribbons and bows for her daughter's almost-invisible hair; she filled drawers with adorable little dresses. She cleaned up her own favorite dolls and added several more, preparing herself to share all sorts of blissful times with her daughter.

The little girl in question, however, had other ideas. She never was a cuddly child and squirmed and wriggled constantly. She crawled and walked early and was always into something—much to her mother's dismay. She delighted in pulling the vacuum cleaner attachments apart and emptied the kitchen cabinets time and time again. The dainty dresses were a nuisance; the baby seemed to have a gift for tearing and staining them.

Things only got more difficult as she grew. She preferred to be called Casey rather than Katy. She had no patience with dolls and tossed them into the darkest corner of her closet or undressed them and scribbled on them with ink; she insisted on "borrowing" her older brother's trucks and guns. Her favorite game was Army, and as soon as she was able, she joined the older boys (despite their howls of protest) in their games, showing an astounding talent for street hockey and climbing trees. She even liked lizards and snakes. Janice tried offering ballet lessons and even gymnastics, but to no avail: Casey refused to be Katy.

The Power of Unconditional Love and Acceptance

DOES JANICE LOVE her child? Undoubtedly she does. But one of the most beautiful ways of expressing love for a child is learning to love *that* child—not the child you wish you had. All parents have dreams for their children, and dreaming is not a bad thing. If we are to encourage our children, though, and build their sense of belonging and self-esteem, we should keep several ideas in mind:

Accepting Your Children As They Are

Children have their own unique temperaments. They have abilities we didn't expect and dreams of their own that don't match ours, and

EFFECTIVE METHODS FOR BUILDING SELF-ESTEEM

- Accepting your children as they are.
- Being patient with your child's development.
- Providing opportunities for success.
- Being aware of self-fulfilling prophecies.

sometimes their behavior is a real disappointment. It is all too easy to compare our offspring with the children down the street, with their cousins, or even with their own siblings and to find them lacking in some way.

We humans are not good at unconditional love, yet children need to be loved unconditionally. We need to learn to love the child we have, which is sometimes easier said than done—and which takes time and patience. Parents need to remember that even the youngest child has an amazing ability to sense her parents' true feelings and attitudes. If she knows she is loved and accepted—if she feels the sense of worth and belonging she craves—she will thrive. If she senses that she doesn't belong, that she is a disappointment or a nuisance, her budding sense of self will wither, and her parents may never get to know the person she could have been. We must try to teach our children to be the best people they can be—not to be someone they are not.

Being Patient with Your Child's Development

Developmental charts are a wonderful way to keep track of the average time span during which children do certain things. The problem is that there are no average children! Children develop—crawl, walk, talk—at their own pace, and many early childhood conflicts stem from parental impatience. Your child will walk and learn toilet training when he's ready; after all, have you ever seen a child crawl off to kindergarten in diapers? If you have serious concerns about your child's development, a word with your pediatrician may set your mind at rest—and save both you and your child a great deal of discouragement.

> We must try to teach our children to be the best people they can be—not to be someone they are not.

Providing Opportunities for Success

Far more powerful than even the most loving and appreciative words are experiences that teach children they are capable, competent people. Begin early to look for your children's special gifts and talents, their abilities and strengths, the things that make them bubble inside. Then give them chances to try those things.

Provide opportunities, too, for them to help you and to take on the little responsibilities they can handle. Early successes and experiences that say "I can do this!" are powerful builders of self-esteem.

Being Aware of Self-Fulfilling Prophecies

We have talked about the importance of changing your attitude about the "terrible twos" and seeing this stage as the "delightful twos." It is interesting to wonder just how terrible the twos would be if parents weren't forever telling each other—and their children—about them. Children have an uncanny ability to live up (or down) to their parents' expectations. If you call your rambunctious toddler a "little monster," don't be surprised if he does his best to be what you expect. In the same way, we can build self-confidence in our children by letting them know we love and accept them and believe in their ability to succeed.

Are our children always going to live out our predictions and expectations? No, of course not. But parents need to remember how powerful our words and opinions are to children. If we tell our children that they're bad, or lazy, or stupid, or clumsy, we shouldn't be surprised that we've reinforced the very behavior we dislike. By the same token, if we look for what's positive in our children, we can choose to reinforce those positives—which leads us to one of the most powerful tools a parent has for building self-esteem in young children: looking for the positive.

TO SPANK OR NOT TO SPANK

Q. When my son was three years old, he was not very bad. The times he was bad, I used to take him to his room and put him on the time-out chair. After a couple of times on the chair, he always did everything right. He was perfect. He still is, now at the age of seven.

Now my daughter is three. She is a horror. She is always bad. I've done everything I can think of. First I tried the chair. It did not work. I tried telling her no, taking away toys, talking about why she was bad, and calling time-outs. I even tried to hug her a lot, saying what she did was bad and she should try not to do it again. The only thing left to do is spank. I never spanked my son, and my mother never spanked me. I don't know if I should. I heard that spanking makes your child bad.

If I do spank, which way is best? Should I use my hand or a belt? Should she be standing or over my knee? I want to do what is best for my daughter.

A. Your question gives us the opportunity to help so many parents who are struggling with the issue of spanking. One of the main purposes of our books is to help parents understand why they should not spank their children—and what to do instead.

Looking for the Positive

THE NEXT TIME your toddler is playing quietly, peek in for just a moment and watch. What do you see? You may notice your child's glowing smile, his ability to build tall towers with his blocks, or his wonderful creativity and imagination. Whatever it is that you see, make a note to share that observation with your child, and then watch what happens. Behavior that is noticed and appreciated is often repeated!

First, parents need to understand that their children are never "bad." It is so important that parents understand developmental appropriateness, Erikson's social and emotional stages of development, and temperament.

We want to emphasize that your daughter is not "bad" and your son is not "perfect." They have different temperaments. Even though your son's temperament is easier to deal with, we worry that he might become an approval junkie or develop low self-esteem. Children are not developing appropriate autonomy and initiative if they do not go through lots of exploring, experimenting, and testing of the rules.

Your daughter sounds very normal, not "bad." The problem is that when punitive methods are used with "normal" children (which includes a wide range of different temperament types), it is the punishment that creates defiance, rebellion, and power struggles. All of the methods you have been using are punitive. You are even turning hugs into punishment by telling her she is bad while hugging her. We're glad you have avoided spanking. Many research studies have shown that over time, spanking creates even worse behavior.

So what should you do? Learn to see every problem as an opportunity for helping your child develop healthy self-esteem and important life skills. Learn to take good care of your own physical and emotional health so that you have the patience and energy to be kind and firm with your challenging toddler.

All human beings long to be appreciated. Young children who are just learning about their world and their place in it have a special need to be encouraged, to have their progress noticed, and to feel they are valuable people.

It is easy in this world of ours to focus on what's wrong. We have no trouble making long lists of what we dislike about ourselves, our spouses, our jobs—and our children. Think for a moment about how you'd feel if your boss at work never did anything but point out your errors and shortcomings. How motivated would you feel to try harder?

Some young children hear a constant litany of "No, no, do it this way" or "How many times do I have to tell you?" or "Here, let me do it." It's no wonder they get discouraged, and as we've already learned, discouragement often leads to misbehavior.

Celebrate the Positive

TAKE A MOMENT sometime soon to make a list of what you really like about your child. Hang the list someplace where you can see it (the refrigerator or the bathroom mirror work well) and add to it when you think of something new. Then find an opportunity each day to appreciate your child for something on the list. Children often bloom amazingly in the steady light of love and encouragement. Don't worry if your child is too young to understand the words you're saying; your warm tone of voice, smiles, and hugs will send the message loud and clear.

Encouragement means noticing progress, not just achievement. It means thanking your small son for picking up most of his cars, even though he missed a few in the corner. It means giving a hug for an attempt on the potty seat, whether or not there was a result. It means smiling with a

> Encouragement says to a child, "I see you trying, and I have faith in you. Keep it up!"

child who has put on her shoes, even though they're on the wrong feet. Encouragement says to a child, "I see you trying, and I have faith in you. Keep it up!"

Looking for the positive in your children and encouraging it is a skill that will serve you throughout childhood and adolescence, and it will help your children to feel good about themselves.

Prevent Problems with Advance Planning

SOME PROBLEMS MAY be prevented when you let your children know how to deal with new situations by taking the time to prepare them for what will happen—which might make the experience much more pleasant for all concerned.

Patsy Tramonto was on her way home from picking up her two-year-old son, Eric, when she decided to stop in at the jewelry shop to get her watch, which had been repaired. She hurried in with Eric tagging along behind her and went straight to the counter to present her claim check.

Eric stood clinging to his mother's coat. He had never been in a shop like this before, and there was a lot to look at. He was gazing about him when suddenly an open display shelf near a window caught his eye and utterly dazzled him.

The late afternoon sunlight was glinting off a collection of the most fascinating objects Eric had ever seen. They were small crystal figures—little animals and people, and even a perfect, tiny castle atop its own crystal mountain, exactly like the one in Eric's favorite storybook—and every movement of Eric's head created rainbows of bright light.

Before Patsy had time to realize what was happening, Eric was off toward the shelf as fast as his short, round legs could carry him. He reached for the wonderful castle, but his small fingers were only strong enough to drag the castle off its shelf and onto the tile floor, where it splintered into pieces.

Eric howled in fright. Patsy was embarrassed, apologetic, and angry—the crystal castle turned out to be shockingly expensive.

What are Patsy's options? Unfortunately, at this point she doesn't have many. She can pay for the broken castle and whisk her small son out to the car, vowing never to take him anywhere again. She can explore with Eric what happened and hope he remembers next time. (Notice that we haven't mentioned punishing Eric; it is doubtful a slap or a time-out would make things any better, especially since Eric had received no guidelines beforehand.)

However, Patsy could have thought things through before entering the store and taken the time to teach. She could have gotten down on Eric's level, perhaps placing her hands gently on his shoulders or taking his hands in hers, and explained that there would be many pretty things in the store but that touching and holding them might break them. Eric could look but not touch. Patsy could have made sure that Eric had something to occupy him while she was busy with the clerk. She probably should have planned on holding his hand anyway, because it is too much to expect that a child will not want to explore at that age, no matter how much teaching takes place. Or she could have decided that discretion was the better part of valor and picked up the watch at a time when Eric could be elsewhere.

Have Faith in Your Child's Ability to Learn

IT IS TEMPTING to tell ourselves that our toddlers and preschoolers are just too young to understand or to do much for themselves, but young children often are more capable than their parents give them credit for. Yes, we need to understand their developmental limitations, and yes, we need to be ready to explain things patiently—many times. But even the youngest child can choose between two shirts to wear or cereal or eggs for breakfast; and even toddlers can put napkins on the dinner table, one at each place. Giving children reasonable responsibilities provides them with opportunities to succeed, to feel capable, and to experience success—the essence of self-esteem.

The Importance of Humor and Hope

THE ABILITY TO laugh and the ability to hope and dream are among the greatest gifts parents can bestow upon their children. From the earliest games of peekaboo with your infant, laughter creates one of the closest bonds between parents and children. Babies and young children are a wonderful source of joy; every day can be an adventure, a chance to laugh and love together. Learning to share a smile, to make funny faces, or to find the humor in situations can carry your family through many tough times.

Rules and limits have their place, and we couldn't function well without them. But try the following experiment sometime: Notice how often you reprimand your child, make a demand of him, or warn against danger or an infraction of the rules. Then count how many times you admire his skills, encourage his explorations, or chuckle together over some amusing incident. Which do you do more often? There needs to be times for relaxing a bit, for allowing a child an extra hug or a few extra minutes of talk before bed, and there are times when the best medicine truly is laughter and play.

First Steps

CHILDREN TAKE MANY first steps—and only a few of them involve walking. Our children need our unqualified support; they need to know we have faith in them. They need opportunities to practice new skills and to take their first steps, no matter how wobbly. They need to know they can make mistakes without risking the loss of their parents' love. When children live in an environment rich with encouragement, are allowed to learn from their mistakes, and experience kind and firm support, they will learn to believe in themselves. Self-esteem must grow within each human's soul and, like any young seedling, it needs nurturing, warmth, and encouragement to thrive.

16

Bonding, Feelings, and Language Development

HAVE YOU EVER watched a mom, dad, or grandparent cradle an infant, gaze down into the baby's face, and coo words of love? What does it all mean to the baby? He can't understand the words—how does he learn to recognize the feelings? How do feelings and vague impressions grow into words, thoughts, and real communication?

The Energy of Feelings

BABIES GENERALLY DO not begin to understand the meanings of words until they are six or seven months of age. Long before that time, however, a baby will turn toward a familiar voice, smile into a parent's face, or reach with delight for favorite people. A bond of love and trust obviously exists, but how has an infant learned to respond to love with pleasure?

Babies and very young children read nonverbal signals and cues to learn about the world of feelings. While an infant may not understand all the complex meanings and concepts contained in the word "love," she does know that the hands that touch and soothe her are gentle and caressing, and the voice that coos and speaks to her is warm and soft. Mom or Dad looks into her eyes and holds her attention. She feels the gentle rain of kisses that tickle her feathery hair. She recognizes familiar smells that communicate the approach of special people and she senses the environment of caring that cherishes her new life. These events convey a feeling of "love" to a young child, and she responds with similar feelings and behavior.

The early weeks and months of life represent a critical period in which a child bonds with the adults who love her; as we learned in chapter 4, her brain is growing (and discarding) connections throughout the first years of life, and the interactions this infant has with the world around her are shaping the way she will grow and develop. Isn't it wonderful that the things we instinctively long to do with babies—touch, tickle, smile, love—are the very things that nurture health and happiness?

Children Absorb Feelings

MOST YOUNG CHILDREN are acutely sensitive to nonverbal communication. In fact, the nonverbal signals we send our children are usually far more powerful than our words. When Mom sits down to nurse feeling annoyed, tired, and cranky, her baby squirms, fusses, and won't settle into nursing. A baby as young as a few weeks of age can sense the tension in her mother's body, feel the rigid muscles in her arms, and hear the thumping of her heart as she lies close to her mom's chest.

Marta Lopez enjoyed quiet mornings and afternoons with her three-week-old baby, Julian. Her husband was at work and the older children were in school. Julian slept much of the time. During his waking moments, after being fed and diapered, he seemed content in his infant seat, watching his mother move about the kitchen. Marta was certain those brief smiles were not gas.

Every day, however, around four o'clock in the afternoon, Julian would start to fuss. Holding and cuddling did not seem to comfort him. Could it be that the baby sensed the stress his mother was feeling about getting dinner on the table and taking care of the children when they came home from school? This seemed to be a reasonable explanation, because the baby would calm down as soon as the busy evening had passed and Marta was able to relax.

> Most young children are acutely sensitive to nonverbal communication. In fact, the nonverbal signals we send our children are usually far more powerful than our words.

Colic

SOME BABIES SEEM to fuss, cry, or scream for no apparent reason for long periods of time. If your baby cries or screams excessively, by all means check with your doctor to be sure there is not a medical reason. Many, many times, however, the doctor will say, "There is nothing seriously wrong. It is just colic." You will find it reassuring to know that your child is not in physical danger, but you will still find it very frustrating when you can't seem to comfort your child.

What is colic, anyway? No one seems to know. It is a catchall description for long periods of crying in babies (who often draw their tiny legs up as though in terrible pain) who seem unconsolable. What can you do? First, remember that it doesn't last forever. Also, don't look for blame. Try to think happy thoughts as you rock, burp, walk the floor with, and offer a pacifier to your little one, holding you arm tightly (but not too tightly) around your little one's tummy. Unfortunately, none of these methods may work for long. It is nice if you have the luxury of a spouse or relative who will take turns trying to help your baby through this miserable time. And for sure, don't worry about household chores that can wait a while, and know that your family can survive on soup and sandwiches.

Create a Calm Atmosphere

A CONTINUING THEME of this book is taking time to enjoy your children. The family won't suffer if you have lots of simple dinners while adjusting to a newcomer to the family (and helping him adjust to you). A calm atmosphere is much more pleasant—and much healthier—for the entire family. You can be even more sensitive to your baby's moods and needs when you slow down and take time to read the energy of all the members of your family.

After a tiring day at work, Sucheta made her daily trek to the child care center to pick up her infant son, Rafael. She hurriedly gathered up the baby and his various belongings, rushed through traffic, and, once home, settled Rafael into his high chair with a snack. She immediately set about fixing dinner. This was the worst hour of the day for mother and son. Rafael fussed, squirmed, and pushed his crackers onto the floor. Sucheta cut herself as she tried to hurry the task of slicing vegetables, spilled too much spice into the recipe, and did not even feel hungry by the time her husband walked through the door. All she felt was despair, exhaustion, and frustration.

Sucheta's husband, Carlos, felt pretty miserable himself, coming home to a squalling baby, undercooked or overcooked meals, and a wife who spent the evening complaining. Watching her husband crush the crackers into the floor when he went over to hug Rafael didn't help Sucheta's mood. One evening, Carlos pushed aside his plate of over-seasoned vegetables. He gazed across the table at his weary wife and began to discuss their miserable evening routine. An understanding smile on his face, he assured Sucheta that he would be glad to make sand-

wiches for both of them if he could come home to a more relaxed wife and child.

Sucheta felt very relieved. She admitted that she felt overwhelmed preparing the elaborate meals they both had enjoyed before Rafael's birth. The next evening, when Sucheta entered the house with Rafael in tow, she put down all of the bags, papers, and toys she had carried in with her. She gave Rafael a big hug and snuggled with him in the rocking chair where they spent the next half hour playing tickling games, cooing and smiling at each other. When Carlos walked through the door, he found Rafael giggling as Sucheta nibbled his toes. Rafael shrieked with laughter as his dad joined in the fun. A short while later, a relaxed family enjoyed peanut butter and jelly sandwiches washed down with hot cups of canned soup. Food hadn't tasted this good in far too long.

Rafael and Sucheta needed time to reconnect each day far more than anyone in the family needed gourmet cooking. By slowing down and allowing time to make the transition from the hectic daily routine to their family time at home, Sucheta was able to tune in to Rafael's needs—and to her husband's. The entire family thrived as the energy in their home improved.

Tantrums: Emotional Meltdowns

THE KITAGAWA FAMILY *walks through the shopping mall together. Two-year-old Nicholas is holding the last bite of his cookie in one hand and a new box of crayons in the other when he spies a display of stuffed Easter bunnies in a store window. He darts off, pointing to the display and dropping the crayons in his haste. Mom and Dad follow him to the store window, retrieving the spilled crayons. They admire the bunnies together. Not surprisingly, Nicholas wants one. "Nicky's bunny!" he says, pointing to a particularly jolly blue specimen. His parents agree that the bunnies look lovely and suggest that perhaps another day he might get one.*

Nicholas, however, isn't satisfied with this answer. He falls to the floor, a writhing mass of pumping legs and pounding fists, and wails with a noisy sincerity that would impress any passing Hollywood producers. Mom glances around in embarrassment while her husband stands over young Nick, telling him to get up right now! Nick lands a random kick on Dad's knee. Dad's voice gets louder than Nick's. Mom, meanwhile, wishes she had a bag to put over her head. Everyone must be watching and thinking what horrible parents they are.

In fact, Nick's parents aren't horrible at all—and neither is Nick. They were sailing along pretty smoothly until the bunnies intervened. Nick's parents responded to him in ways that did not invite a power struggle; they avoided saying an outright "no" and had already given him several special treats that afternoon. So why did Nick throw a tantrum? Is he a spoiled brat? Does he just need a good spanking? No. The most likely answer is that Nick threw a tantrum "just because."

Tantrums are loud, highly visible, and embarrassing. They are also quite normal. Young children have all of the same feelings adults do. They feel sad, happy, and frustrated, but they lack both the words for those feelings and the skills (and impulse control) to cope with them. They just know that some strong force comes along and *boom*—they lose it. This entirely normal situation sets the stage for the thunderstorm we call a tantrum. When the air gets too heavy with emotions, children spark lightning bolts, boom out frustration, and spout cloudbursts of tears. Then they feel better—oh, so much better.

Once adults understand why children's overloaded senses sometimes flash into tantrums, they can quit feeling responsible for them. Sometimes, no matter what we say or do, children will get overwhelmed and throw tantrums. Adults can learn not to add to the chaos. It is too bad that Nick's dad got into the act by throwing a tantrum of his own. Nick's tantrum will pass quickly, but it may take his parents—now carrying their howling son to the car—longer to recover their equilibrium.

Weathering the Storm: What to Do During (and After) a Tantrum

TANTRUMS MAY BE normal, but that doesn't mean parents will enjoy them. What can parents and caregivers do to help a child through the storm? Try the following during a tantrum.

- *Provide a safe environment.* As long as a child is not hurting others or damaging anything, simply provide a safe place to wait out the storm.

- *Provide damage control.* While tantrums may be part of living with young children, damage and injury need not be. It may be wise to move a child to another, safer location, or, if you are in a public place, to a more private corner. Without yelling or lecturing, calmly move any objects that may be thrown or damaged out of your child's reach.

- *Do not try to "fix" a tantrum or coax a child with rewards.* Offering to give a child a disputed item teaches him that tantrums make good tools for getting his way. Remember that tantrums are normal but giving in to demands for toys or special service will only earn you more tantrums. Remain kind, calm, and firm, and let the storm blow over.

> Once adults understand why children's overloaded senses sometimes flash into tantrums, they can quit feeling responsible for them. Sometimes, no matter what we say or do, children will get overwhelmed and throw tantrums.

- *Don't get hooked by your child's behavior.* As much as possible, try to ignore the tantrum. If you are at home and your child is safe, you may want to go into the next room or pick up a book to look at. This sends the message that you aren't angry but neither will you let yourself be manipulated by kicking and screaming.

After the tantrum, try the following.

- *Allow emotions to settle.* Give children and adults time to recover. Allow yourself and your child a quiet moment to cool down and catch your breath. Tantrums can be scary and disturbing for everyone, and you'll do better work as a parent if you've had time to calm down.

- *Offer support.* Children may need a hug after such a powerful emotional storm. Tears and sniffles often follow tantrums as the child clears out the overload of emotions. A wordless, comforting hug may help both of you feel better.

- *Help your child make amends.* When everyone has calmed down, any damage should be addressed. Thrown items can be picked up, torn papers gathered and discarded, or pillows stacked back on the bed or sofa. Adults may offer to help a child with these tasks.

   It may also be appropriate to help your child repair additional damage, such as a broken toy. Recognize your child's abilities and development and don't expect things she can't do, but allowing her to squeeze some glue, run the Dustbuster, or put tape on a torn book may help her feel a sense of self-control again and give her a very real way to learn about apologizing and making things right.

- *Forgive and forget—and plan ahead.* Once the tantrum is over and the mess has been cleaned up, let it go. Concentrate on building relationship and trust and, if you can, on recognizing what led up to the tantrum. Prevention is often the best way of dealing with children's thunderstorms. Tantrums may happen when children have missed naps or meals, are in unfamiliar surroundings, or are coping with stressed-out adults. Understanding your child's temperament and daily rhythms will help you both avoid many of these outbursts.

Baby-Size Overload

Q. *I know this sounds unbelievable (at least it does to me), but my eleven-month-old daughter screams and kicks like she's having a tantrum. It's loud and blood-curdling! I always walk away and let her scream when she does it, because I don't want to reinforce the negative behavior. She only screams a little while, mostly when she's going to bed. Is there anything else I should be doing to discourage this behavior? Is this normal behavior for an eleven-month-old?*

A. What you describe sounds more like a child who is just feeling overwhelmed. Children do not have many tools for stress management. Crying is a way for them to release tension, which is a normal part of everyday life. A tired baby actually might just want to be left alone to calm down.

The Martinez family discovered the importance of alone time with one of their children. Their attempts to soothe their youngest daughter with walking, singing, and stroking only made her cry harder. When they would finally lay her down, she seemed relieved. She would cry a minute or two, then relax and fall asleep. Their well-meaning stimulation actually prolonged her distress.

Remember, crying is communication for infants, not misbehavior. Each of us needs to learn to interpret the message our child is sending. Crying does not always mean the same thing. It is not reinforcing negative behavior to respond to a baby's cries. We must respond so we can learn what the crying means.

What About Head Banging?

Q. *I have three girls, ages five, three, and two. They are great kids! I am wondering how I can stop my two-year-old from having temper tantrums. I've already tried ignoring the action. If she doesn't get what she wants, she falls to the floor and begins to bang her head, sometimes very hard. I don't know what to do. Please help.*

A. Tantrums, head banging, holding breath—all are very common in young children who aren't getting their way. All are very upsetting to concerned parents. Sometimes these behaviors are the means by which your child vents her frustration. Your two-year-old may also have discovered that these behaviors "work"—in other words, they get her something she believes she needs: the object of her demands, or your attention and involvement. Two-year-olds are programmed by their emotional development to want independence and the right to make their own choices—but obviously, we're the parents and that's still our job.

You're on the right track when you try to ignore her. If you're worried that your daughter may bruise herself by banging her head on something hard, pick her up and without saying anything move her to a softer spot (the carpet, her bed, a pillow). You might try saying, "I'd like to work on this with you, but we can't talk when you're so upset." Then let her know you are available when she's calmed down. Make sure she's in a safe place and take some deep breaths to calm yourself. It will take time, but if you're kind and firm, she'll get the message that you can't be manipulated by tantrums, tears, and threats. Hang in there!

Reflective Listening: Giving Names to Feelings

CHILDREN CONSTANTLY SEND nonverbal messages. Their facial expressions, gestures, and behavior provide clues to vigilant adults about what they are feeling. An eighteen-month-old child cannot tell you, "I'm feeling tired, confused, and a bit frustrated that I can't reach the cookie jar"; he doesn't have the words to express such a complicated sequence of thoughts and feelings. What you might hear are wails and shrieks accompanied by a toy thrown to the ground, a crumpled-up face, and a small body collapsing on the floor.

A parent might react with understandable frustration of her own and may express that frustration with harsh words. Or she can choose to help her child understand his feelings, give them a label that will help him to identify them in the future, and open the door to a way of dealing with the situation at hand.

Mom might respond like this: "Pumpkin, I can see that you feel angry because you can't reach the cookie jar. I feel angry when I can't do something, too. I'll bet we could figure out a way to solve this problem. What do you think?"

Once a child's feelings are named, validated, and understood, he usually feels better and is more willing to work on solutions. In this instance, Mom helped her son figure out that he could push a chair over to the counter so he could reach the cookie jar. They also decided to fill the cookie jar with healthy snacks, such as popcorn, crackers, or raisins, so he could help himself anytime.

Your Child's Perspective

WHEN HER NEW *neighbor stopped by for a visit, Elana's normally outgoing toddler became very clingy. Elana felt embarrassed when he refused to say hello to the visitor. She kept tugging at him to step forward, becoming more upset with him as the visit progressed. When Elana looked down in exasperation, she caught sight of the look in her son's eyes and realized that he was feeling both nervous and uncomfortable in this situation. She acted on her intuition, gathering him into her*

> Once a child's feelings are named, validated, and understood, he usually feels better and is more willing to work on solutions.

arms and hugging him tightly. She ceased her attempts to get him to greet their visitor.

As soon as her son felt reassured, his natural curiosity took over. He began peeking his head out from Elana's shoulder and was able to flash a big grin and shake hands when the neighbor extended her hand to him.

When we take the time to see the world through our child's eyes, we may get a very different view. Children usually have good reasons for their behavior; wise adults learn to take time to understand their child's perceptions and feelings.

Understanding Feelings Is Not the Same As Permissiveness

THERE IS, PERHAPS, no emotion that causes more problems for parents than a child's anger. Young children express anger in ways their parents find alarming: temper tantrums, throwing objects, yelling, hitting, kicking, even biting. (Biting is a common way for children who aren't yet verbally skilled to express anger or frustration; see chapter 9 for more about biting.) All human beings have feelings—lots of them!—and all of us, adults and children, need ways to express and understand our feelings.

Does this mean parents should tolerate hitting, yelling, or kicking as acceptable expressions of anger? Of course not. Actions that harm others (or oneself) are not acceptable ways of expressing feelings. Parents and teachers can make an effort to get into the young child's world and understand it. They can practice reflective listening to validate and clarify feelings, and they can then teach children to express their anger (which may be completely justified) in acceptable ways.

Children learn so much by watching. We model how to deal with strong feelings when we stand quietly and take some deep breaths instead of reacting immediately to upsets, when we respond to a child who tries to hit us without hitting him back, or when we walk over to a child, get down on his eye level, and request that he stop a behavior rather than hollering at him to do so from across the room.

Children learn about anger by:

- Watching how adults behave when angry

- Experiencing how others treat them when angry

- Learning to identify feelings of anger within themselves

It is tempting to respond to anger with anger—to join in the yelling, send kids off to a punitive time-out, or otherwise try to fix the situation at hand. These responses usually escalate the conflict and destroy any opportunity there might have been to teach, to understand, or to find a workable solution to the problem.

Remember, your little one does not have the same understanding of anger that you do. He needs your help both to identify this feeling and to learn to manage and express it in appropriate ways. How can parents and caregivers help an angry child?

Use Words to Label the Feelings

Using a calm voice, "reflect" the feeling to your child. You might say, "Boy, you look angry! I see that your chin is sticking out, your eyebrows are all scrunched up, and your fists are clenched." Giving

How should you react when your child shows anger?

- Use words to label the feelings.
- Validate the feelings.
- Provide appropriate ways for your child to express his feelings.

these clues helps a child make the connection between what he feels and how he behaves. Obviously, real understanding takes time, but it's never too soon to start.

Validate the Feelings

There is no such thing as a "wrong" feeling—something many adults have yet to learn! We usually have our feelings—whatever they are—for very good reasons. Begin teaching your child that his feelings are always okay, but some actions are not.

Provide Appropriate Ways for Your Child to Express His Feelings

What might an angry toddler do? Well, it might help to pound a lump of clay or a pillow, roar like a dinosaur, scribble on paper with markers, run around the backyard, or punch a "bop bag." Parents usually discover that anger expressed in healthy ways dissipates much more quickly; in fact, they often find themselves giggling with the same toddler who was so furious only moments before. Try saying, "It's okay to be mad—I'd feel pretty mad, too, if I were you. It's not okay to hit me or hurt yourself. What would help you feel better?" Remember, we usually do better when we feel better. Lessons learned now about recognizing and managing feelings will benefit your child his entire life.

> Begin teaching your child that his feelings are always okay, but some actions are not.

A Word About "Blankies" and Other Security Objects

CLOSELY TIED TO a child's feelings of trust and security is one accessory of young childhood that has passed into folklore: the security blanket. Linus, in the cartoon strip *Peanuts,* carries his everywhere, even using it to zap his obnoxious older sister. Children the world over rely on scraps of blanket, favorite stuffed animals, or imaginary friends to help them feel secure—and parents the world over often wonder if it's healthy to allow them to do so.

With a little thought, it's easy to understand how intimidating a place this world of ours can be to a very young child. A child's attachment to his blankie can be very strong; it often has its own feel and taste, and a child can usually tell if an attempt is made to replace or switch the favorite object. Many parents have had the alarming experience of leaving a teddy or blankie at the grocery store or in a motel, then having to make an emergency return trip with an hysterical child.

Feelings of insecurity and fear, while they can be upsetting for parents, are like all other emotions: they are just feelings and can be handled with reflective listening, warmth, and understanding. If sleeping with a special blanket or a stuffed animal helps a child relax and feel cozy, is there truly any harm?

Some children never adopt a blankie or stuffed animal, preferring instead to suck on their thumbs or on a pacifier. Monica was sure that children would not suck their thumbs if they had plenty of opportunity to suck at the breast. However, the one child she had nursed on demand sucked her thumb until she was six. Monica had to admit, "So much for that theory!"

Pacifiers can be a wonderful way to help an infant satisfy her need to suck, and they can provide security (and peace) during times of upset or stress. In fact, children who appear to have given up their thumb or pacifier often resume the habit if the family moves, if they change child care settings or caregivers, or if there is some other upheaval in their lives. Most parents eventually wonder if thumb sucking or using a pacifier is wise, especially as a child grows older, but the problem is more the adult's attitude than the child's well-being.

If you have concerns about sucking needs, especially where teeth and orthodontia are concerned, you may be able to put your fears at rest by talking to a pediatric dentist. As a general rule, the less fuss adults make, the sooner the issue tends to be resolved. As they grow older, children often are willing to restrict use of their security objects to bedtime or nap time, especially if they have experienced understanding and acceptance from their parents. Most children, left to themselves, eventually give up their blankies or pacifiers of their own free will, usually by the age of six.

"Maria's blankie sort of fell apart," said Carol. "It literally disintegrated until she was down to a few shredded pieces. It became a bother for her to find these fragments and so the blankie passed quietly into history. Actually, I gathered up a couple of these pieces and tucked them into my jewelry box. I couldn't part with them. I plan on adding them to a quilt for my grandchild someday." It is amazing how many parents who lamented their child's attachment to a blanket keep a small scrap as a memento long after their child has abandoned it!

Language Skills and Communication

IT CAN BE frustrating to try to communicate with and understand a young child who can't yet express his feelings and ideas—and it must be frustrating to be that child as well! Like most other developmental skills, the acquisition of language takes place at different rates for different children, and how comfortable your child is with using words will affect the way he behaves and expresses his feelings.

As we've already mentioned, for young children biting is often an expression of frustration that can't be vented any other way. A child may be subconsciously thinking, "If I can't use my mouth to speak, I'll use it to communicate another way!"

Most parents eagerly await their children's first words, sharing them with friends and family and recording them for posterity in baby books and journals. We smile over their innocent mispronunciations and other manglings of the language, and we rejoice when they can make themselves understood consistently.

By the age of seven or eight months, most babies understand the meanings of a few words. By three years of age, most children understand ordinary, conversational language, although they may not be able to produce it themselves. Children often understand many words by the age of one year, but they may say only a few before they are two years old, despite endless coaching from Mom and Dad. If your child seems alert and responds well to you, chances are that all is well, even if she doesn't have much to say—yet!

It is worth knowing that children learn language best by being spoken to often and given lots of opportunities to respond and to practice their budding conversational skills. Holding a running conversation as you stroll down the grocery aisle about the bright red apples, whether or not you are out of peanut butter, or if salmon would be nice for dinner tonight does not mean you expect your four-month-old to take over shopping anytime soon. This kind of conversation allows his ear to become accustomed to language, in the same way that those age-old nursery rhymes teach children to recognize the rhythms and sounds of spoken words—and to duplicate them when the time is right. No matter how exhausting it can be, a toddler's endless stream of "why" and "how come" questions should be answered calmly. As one three-year-old reminded his exasperated mom, "That's how little boys learn!"

The Importance of Talk

LANGUAGE—THE WORDS we speak and the way we speak them—shapes our very thoughts. Most researchers believe that acquiring language

No matter how exhausting it can be, a toddler's endless stream of "why" and "how come" questions should be answered calmly. As one three-year-old reminded his exasperated mom, "That's how little boys learn!"

skills is critical to the development of thinking, problem solving, and higher reasoning. Unfortunately, educators and researchers also tell us that the ability to use language well is declining rapidly among today's children. They are less able to learn, to think, and to write. Frighteningly enough, their brains aren't developing the connections necessary to function well academically, to appreciate literature, and to write a logical paragraph. Why?

The biggest culprit probably is our hectic, harried lifestyle and the ways we choose to use what time we do have with our children. Time in which to sit and read or to talk with one another is all too limited. Children are propped in front of videos and television programs while parents fix dinner, do chores, or work at home. Children may learn the *Barney* theme song or recognize letters and numbers, but contrary to most parents' belief they do not learn language. The sort of listening required to watch television is passive; children aren't getting the opportunity to listen actively to stories, nursery rhymes, or real conversation, and they don't get to practice how to respond, learning in the process that conversation is a two-way process.

What talking adults say to children is, all too often, strictly functional. "Get into your pajamas," "Eat your dinner," or "Don't hit your sister" may be all the conversation our little ones hear. Perhaps most sadly, many children spend most of their waking hours in child

What are the best ways to encourage language skills?

- Talk to children
- Encourage children to "talk back"
- Read lots of books
- Turn off the television—at least most of the time

care centers where overburdened caregivers might value silence, not budding language skills.

Teaching Language

WE UNDERSTAND NOW that there are important time frames in which young children's brains are programmed to learn language. Many parents believe that there will be time "later on" to teach words and language skills, but most language learning takes place in the first three years of life. What can parents and caregivers do to give little ones the best chance of learning language now—and succeeding in school later on?

Talk to Children

Parents seem to have an instinctive understanding of the sort of verbal play that infants and young children need. Word games, peekaboo, and pat-a-cake are actually wonderful ways to acquaint babies with the mysteries of language. Let children hear your voice; speak to them often. Sing the old-fashioned nursery rhymes. What you say is probably less important than giving them the opportunity to experiment with sounds and words. As your children get older, telling stories is a wonderful way to help children follow a story line, learn to separate word meanings from pictures, and stretch their ability to visualize and imagine, all crucial parts of later learning.

Encourage Children to "Talk Back"

No, we don't mean that sort of back talk. But it is important to give children the opportunity to talk to you, to other adults, and to other children. At first, children's "speech" may consist of single words and gestures, but as you encourage them ("what" and "how" questions are a wonderful way), their ability to speak to you and to communicate thoughts and feelings will grow. Adults sometimes grow impatient with young children and rush to finish their sentences for them; do your best to remain patient and give them space and time to communicate.

Read Lots of Books

Reading to young children may be the most helpful activity parents can do. Even babies can be propped in your lap to gaze at the pages of a colorful board book, and toddlers usually love to cuddle up and read stories. As you read, become the characters: change your voice and provide sound effects, and encourage your child to do the same. Don't rely entirely on picture books; read books that have more text and encourage your child to form his own pictures for the words you read.

Reading can become a favorite part of a toddler's day, and young children usually are eager to soak up the new worlds books can open. Three-year-old Kevin's mother was astonished when he "read" a favorite Berenstain Bears book to her one day. He had memorized the words, the voices—and the right place to turn the pages. Barbara was thirteen months old when her favorite aunt sat down to read a book about flowers with her. Barbara gazed intently at the picture, pulled the book into her hands, and put her nose against the page for a long sniff. Her aunt was amazed at this demonstration of just how well Barbara understood the connection between the printed page and the real object it represented.

As your child grows older, share with her the books you loved or check with friends for titles their children have enjoyed. Make reading together, a chapter or two a night, part of your bedtime routine. Many parents find that this cozy ritual lasts far beyond toddlerhood and provides a time of warmth and closeness for years to come.

Turn Off the Television— at Least Most of the Time

As we learned in chapter 4, television may actually change the way a child's brain functions. At the very least we know that watching television is entirely passive; children who watch a great deal of TV show less creativity in their play. Balance may be a realistic goal; a little *Sesame Street* or the beloved Disney videos are welcome entertainment for young children. But be sure there is more than enough time for books, music, play, and conversation as well.

It is sobering to realize how much learning takes place in the first three years of life—and that we imperfect parents and caregivers are responsible for most of it. It may be helpful to remember that most language development takes place naturally, *when parents and caregivers make time to play and talk with children.* As we've said so many times before, raising and caring for active young children is a challenging job, and providing opportunities for them to learn about feelings, words, and the world around them may seem like just one more burdensome thing to do. Take a deep breath, relax, and remind yourself to enjoy these years. It's never too late—or too soon—to begin.

PART SIX

Keeping Your Family Strong

Care and Support for Parents and Children

HAPPY DAY
CHILD CARE

No matter how capable and competent we are as parents and caregivers, we usually have trouble taking care of children entirely on our own. Most adults must work, either in or out of the home, and for most families child care of some sort is a fact of life. Adults, too, need nurturing and encouragement. We have questions, and we have moments when our patience evaporates. All parents occasionally feel stress; all will question their effectiveness from time to time.

In this last section, we will explore the world of child care and help parents select a caregiver both they and their children can feel secure with. We will also suggest ways that parents can care for their own physical and emotional health—it's an important task and one that most of us overlook from time to time. Our families will thrive when we and our children feel nurtured, supported, and safe.

17

Who's Watching the Kids?

Choosing—and Living with— Child Care

IN THOUSANDS AND thousands of homes across this nation, each working day begins with the ritual of packing lunches, gathering backpacks and jackets, and driving the children to their child care facility. Some children go to relatives' homes, while others spend the day in large centers with many other children. Some receive excellent care, opportunities to learn and grow, and have lots of fun, while others spend the hours bored, lonely, or neglected. And in thousands and thousands of homes, parents suffer confusion, regret, or doubt about the wisdom of leaving their children in someone else's care. For thousands of other parents, child care simply is not an option. Listen for a moment to the voices of two of these parents.

Q. *I have read that you feel that mothers who work do not have a negative effect on their children. Could you please expand on this? Radio programs, newspaper articles, and magazines offer such conflicting advice that I feel really confused. At the present time it is not possible for me to quit my job because my husband is bedridden with a back injury.*

My son spends about nine hours a day at child care. Will this have a negative impact on my son? Do you have any suggestions or advice? I feel terribly guilty. I love my son more than anything and want to be with him, but I can't be. Thank you.

Q. *My neighbor just came by for a visit. Her son attends child care three days a week while she works at a part-time job. Joseph is two months younger than my son, and yet Joseph can count, write his name, and knows all his colors, while my son does none of these things. I am a full-time mom at home with our son all day. I feel really inadequate whenever my neighbor and her son visit. I am worried that my son will be behind when it is time for him to begin school. Should I put him in a preschool? I'm sure my neighbor thinks I am not too bright for just staying home all the time.*

A. Most people hold strong opinions about who should care for young children. The authors believe that where or from whom a child receives care matters less than the quality of the care itself. "Good" child care supports the development of healthy self-esteem, emotional well-being, learning and brain growth, and the ability to form healthy relationships with other people.

Many mothers seem to feel guilty whether they stay at home or not. Feeling guilty does not do anyone the least bit of good. Neither does being judgmental. Everyone makes choices based on his or her own situation and beliefs. Young children love to be with their parents, and we know that the bond of mother, father, and child is vital. But this bond does not thrive only in isolation. Children can learn and grow in many different settings.

Is Child Care Harmful?

ONE CHILD CARE provider shares her family's story:

I stayed home with our two oldest children throughout their first three years. When our second child turned three, we opened a child care

*center. We have four children. Our two youngest children were in the
center from their earliest days and our second child from just past the age
of three. In many ways, our two youngest children
had the best of both worlds. They were with their
parents, since both their dad and I worked at the
child care center, and they also took part in a wonderful child care program each day.*

*All four of our children are thriving today. In
addition, the other children we cared for in those
early years of our center's existence are now young
adults; some are parents themselves. They frequently stop by to visit and
reminisce with us, and more than one has told us that their time at our
center helped them experience subsequent successes in their lives. They
are loving, capable, and responsible people.*

Children can learn and grow in many different settings.

There are all kinds of conflicting studies, attitudes, and theories
about child care. The experience offered above gives a long-range
perspective and one that includes raising children both in and out of
the home. Many people may contend, "It isn't working outside the
home when you are able to take your children with you." That is not
the point. These children still had challenges to deal with, such as
sharing their parents with other children. Some parents work at
home and deal with interruption issues. Parents who work away from
the home and can't take their children with them
find that life provides other challenges. Every life
situation presents challenges that can be dealt
with successfully if we have effective attitudes
and skills.

Every life situation presents chal-
lenges that can be dealt with successfully if we have effective attitudes and skills.

Being a stay-at-home parent offers many
rewards for both parents and their youngsters. So
do the experiences available in quality child care
programs. Being home with a child offers no
magical outcomes; it does not make anyone a perfect
parent or guarantee a child's ideal development.

Work and Child Care: What Are They?

PEOPLE WORK IN many different ways. Women work in and out of the home all the time. Beverly writes a column for a local newspaper and brings two-year-old Jason to a child care center near her office. Mary Beth puts together the weekly church newsletter, spending two mornings a week at the church office while her son plays with other children during the women's Bible study play group. Both of these moms "work" (volunteers are working moms, too).

Child care refers to more than just home- or center-based programs. Grandma takes care of baby Lori while Mom volunteers as a reading tutor at her oldest daughter's elementary school. Elizabeth takes her infant to the neighbor's house every morning when she leaves for her job as a receptionist at a large hospital. Her neighbor watches her own infant, Elizabeth's daughter, and several older children who arrive after school each day. Jean entertains her younger brother after she comes home from high school so their father can process tax returns in his home-based accountant's office upstairs. Child care has many faces.

It seems that the definition of "working parent" often gets narrowed to include only people who are paid, who use providers other than family members, or who work for more than a few hours each week. In fact, moms and dads do all kinds of work and their children spend all or part of each day in other people's care. Often, those children enjoy a wide variety of life experiences.

Child Care: A Global Perspective

IT IS NORMAL to view situations through the lens of our own culture and history. Over the course of time, however, few cultures have expected mothers to stay home all alone to care for tiny children.

Most often children have been cared for by older siblings, aunts, and nearby or resident grandparents.

The popular phrase "It takes a village to raise a child" comes from rural Africa. In this context, the "village" is a child's blood relatives, neighbors, and community or tribal members. East Indian families typically contain several generations in one household. Some cultures in Africa or the Middle East allow a man to take more than one wife. These households might include several wives as well as stepbrothers and stepsisters, all of whom participate in caring for children. In many Asian countries, women move in with their husband's family when they marry. In Native American culture, it is traditional for children to be raised by many "aunties," some not related by blood at all. In all these cultures, children receive care from an extended family of friends and relatives. They might view our belief that mothers and fathers should raise children without outside advice or help as a form of insanity!

Choices

TAKE A MOMENT to read the stories of some of the parents who bring their children to child care facilities.

Stephanie is grateful that a child care facility is located in her office building. Her son will be six months old next week, and the proximity of the child care center makes it possible for Stephanie to continue nursing him, something that is very important to her. She hurries downstairs on her breaks and lunch hour, eager to cuddle with her son. Stephanie was not married when she became pregnant, and the baby's father does not support her, but Stephanie chose to continue her pregnancy and raise her son as a single parent. She is devoted to her son and works hard to provide him with a loving home. Divorce, single parenthood, and even welfare reform leave few options for a woman raising a child without outside financial support.

Bernadette drops two-year-old Mitchell off at his child care just before eight o'clock each morning. Mitchell's dad works nights and sleeps during the day. Their combined incomes barely cover the cost of their one-bedroom apartment. Even with subsidies from the city to help pay child care costs, Bernadette must spend an extra two hours each day commuting by bus because car and insurance payments are beyond their limited budget.

Roger and Jennifer both hold well-paying jobs with the same company Stephanie works for. Jennifer tried staying home with three-year-old Todd but found she missed the stimulation of her job. The harder she tried to be a stay-at-home mom, the grumpier she became—and the angrier she became when Todd misbehaved. Perhaps, she worries, she just wasn't meant to be a full-time mom. She and Roger love Todd dearly, but Jennifer has discovered that she is a much better parent when she isn't cranky and irritable from being confined all day with an active toddler. She struggles with guilt, but she and Roger truly believe that Todd is happier and healthier at the child care center, climbing on the equipment and playing with his many friends. Jennifer thrives at her job and can better enjoy Todd's delightful antics. She feels more confident in her new role of mother.

Tyneesha, on the other hand, has two children who do not go to child care. The children share a bedroom so that the spare room can be rented to a college student. The rental income makes it possible for Tyneesha to stay at home with four-month-old Erica and three-year-old Malcolm. Tyneesha's husband has a civilian job at the naval shipyard in town. His commute takes an hour each day, but homes located closer to the base are out of their price range. The long days wear Tyneesha out and sometimes the demands of her two tiny youngsters make her want to scream. On other days, her heart melts just looking at them and she offers prayers of thanksgiving for the time she gets to spend with them.

Stay-at-home parents find that one-on-one daily contact with an infant, toddler, or preschooler includes magical moments of discovery, tender times of sharing, and precious memories for both parent and child. Staying home also means moments of despair when toilets overflow from being fed whole rolls of toilet paper by a curious toddler, episodes of hysterical raging when a preschooler's screeching wakes up his sleeping baby sister, or feeling helpless when a defiant toddler throws his blocks across the room after refusing to pick them up. Being home with a child does not make anyone a perfect parent, nor does it guarantee a child's ideal development. Neither does child care offer all the answers.

Working parents face lots of pressure and criticism, and they may feel enormous guilt about being away from their little ones. Choosing to work or stay home is a complicated decision, and there is rarely a simple "right" or "wrong" answer. Each of us must face our own reality and make the best decisions we can.

> Being home with a child does not make anyone a perfect parent, nor does it guarantee a child's ideal development. Neither does child care offer all the answers.

Many women want nothing more than to stay at home with their babies. In a perfect world, that choice would be possible for everyone—but in the real world, harsh reality intervenes. Parents who choose to stay at home to raise a child, to forgo career and financial rewards, or to accept a simpler lifestyle deserve recognition, respect, and support. Those who work deserve the same. The issue is not whether we agree with our neighbor's choice but whether we have made the best choice for ourselves and for our children.

Old and New Extended Family

HAVING EXTENDED FAMILY members to care for our children has become increasingly rare for many of us. In our book *Positive Discipline for Preschoolers* we suggest that today's child care programs may take on the role of the historic extended family. When this happens, it is child care at its best.

Families need the support of many people when tackling the task of raising young children, and a "good" child care program provides helpers with lots of knowledge, experience, and information. When Ellen's daughter was diagnosed with asthma, the child care teacher at her daughter's center provided reassurance and introduced Ellen to other families whose children had similar problems. Juan's mother panicked when she discovered a rash on his stomach. One look by the center director confirmed another case of chicken pox. Juan's mother got the information she needed to care for him and learned what to expect and about how long the illness might take to run its course, thanks to the director's experience.

Janell has few friends with young children. Her own daughter, Nicole, arrived only a few weeks ago after more than a year of paperwork, delays, and waiting lists; Nicole turned four months old on her adoption day. Janell is a single parent who needs to work, and the child care center has proven invaluable as a source of support for her newly formed family. Other families at the child care center provide the sense of community, sibling-like relationships, and social gatherings that Janell and Nicole need. Several other children at the center were adopted, and one of them came from the same country as Nicole. This family quickly formed a close bond with Janell and Nicole, planning get-togethers and supporting each other as they and their new infants got to know one another.

> The frequent absence of a nearby extended family may create isolation for moms at home. Even if they have family nearby, moms need encouragement, social contact, and support.

Stay-at-home moms also need support. The common absence of a nearby extended family may create isolation for moms at home. Even if they have family nearby, moms need encouragement, social contact, and support. We have covered the broader issue of support systems for both working and stay-at-home mothers in chapters 1 and 3 and will discuss it further in chapter 18.

Encouragement and Early Intervention

BAILEY GETS BUSSED *every afternoon to child care. Each morning, he participates in a special program for youngsters with a variety of developmental delays. Bailey's mom, Shirley, had wondered why he seemed to have such a hard time learning new skills. Being a first-time mom, Shirley assumed her own lack of experience caused her to worry needlessly about Bailey, but only a few weeks after Bailey began attending his child care, the director asked to meet with Shirley. The staff was concerned about Bailey's development. Together, the center and Shirley sought outside help. Shirley and the staff were right to feel concerned. Bailey was delayed in speech, motor, and other communication skills. Specific problems were identified, and a few months later Bailey was admitted to a special morning program at the university. Without the center's experienced staff, caring support, and knowledge, Shirley might not have gotten Bailey the early intervention he needed.*

Early intervention is usually more effective in helping children with delays "catch up" than that provided to older children. The experience of caregivers offers opportunities to identify children and families in need of special assistance. This type of identification might not happen in all centers, but if a caregiver expresses a concern about your child's development, it is wise to pursue the matter. Each caregiver has the experience of seeing many children and over time becomes better able to identify when things are amiss.

Kyle's parents have filed for divorce. He now sees his dad only on weekends. He and his mom have moved into an apartment, and Kyle's mom has to work longer hours than before. The only thing that remains unchanged in Kyle's life is his child care center. Kyle sees the same faces every morning, recognizes the circle songs, and knows that snack time comes just after story time. With everything else in his life shifting like quicksand, he feels safe, secure, and reassured at his child care center.

"Good" child care goes beyond simply providing a place for children to be cared for in their parents' absence. Early intervention, consistency during times of change, and support for families are wonderful ways in which child care programs can enhance the quality of children's lives. What about child care that is less than ideal? What about all those horror stories in the newspapers and on the television news shows? Obviously, not all child care is created equally—and not all of it benefits children. How can parents know that they're leaving their little ones in competent, qualified hands? What makes for "good" child care?

"Good" Child Care

IF YOU ARE one of the many parents who needs to find regular care for your child, you need to consider a number of factors. Don't

---

CHILD CARE CHECKLIST

Identify quality child care using the following indicators:

1. The center or home has
   - Current licenses displayed
   - A low rate of staff turnover
   - Local, state, and/or national accreditation

2. The staff is
   - Well-trained in early childhood development and care
   - Working as a team
   - Staying up-to-date through training programs
   - Adequately paid

be in a rush to choose: Be sure to visit several different child care programs. What do you see? Are the children happy? Do they move around the center confidently? Do the caregivers get down on the child's eye level to talk with him? Is the artwork displayed low enough for children to see it or only at adult eye level? Is the building clean? Are there visible safety hazards? Do the caregivers look cheerful or frazzled? (Do remember that even the best teachers can have tough days!) Does the equipment provided allow children to play freely, to dress up, to learn, and to be active? Or are children expected to be quiet, sit still, and "be good"?

Find out if the program is licensed and by whom. Does the center pass city licensing requirements, health department codes, and fire safety requirements?

Some child care programs are beginning to offer "online monitoring." These programs allow centers to install cameras in several places throughout the building. Software is available for parents to

3. Discipline is
   - Nonpunitive
   - Kind and firm at the same time
   - Designed to help children learn important life skills

4. Consistency shows
   - In the curriculum
   - In the way problems are handled
   - In day-to-day center management

5. Safety is demonstrated by the
   - Physical setting
   - Program health policies
   - Preparedness for emergencies

install in their computer so they can periodically see what is happening in the day care program. Parents can "visit" occasionally during the day, see exactly what their child is doing, and see their child in action. Other programs are moving to the Internet by designing home pages on which they post weekly information, share anecdotes, and scan in pictures of daily events, field trips, or special moments. Whatever the bells and whistles, trust your "gut" instinct before leaving your child in anyone else's care.

Child care requires top-notch support: Do not economize! Choosing child care should not involve bargain hunting—you're likely to get exactly what you pay for.

Good Child Care: How Can I Tell?

PARENTS SOMETIMES LOOK at lists of qualities and requirements for good child care and feel overwhelmed. You may be wondering how you will ever know if the facility you are considering meets these standards. There is a relatively simple solution: ask. Child care is an important decision, and your confidence as a parent will influence your child's comfort with and response to her new setting. Don't hesitate to ask for all of the information you need to make an educated decision. If a center or provider seems reluctant to answer your questions or to allow you to observe personnel in action, it's probably wise to look elsewhere!

> If a center or provider seems reluctant to answer your questions or to allow you to observe personnel in action, it's probably wise to look elsewhere!

You might want to copy the checklist above and take it with you when you visit prospective child care facilities. We discuss each of the points in the following sections.

The Center or Home

Most states or cities require centers and homes to meet a variety of licensing requirements. Seeing licenses posted tells you the requirements were met. Be sure to check dates to be sure that licenses are current (although many states are so backlogged that long intervals between licensing are common).

Centers with low staff turnover indicate that staff members are well-treated, receive fair compensation, enjoy their work, and feel supported by the center's administration. When staff members do not receive decent wages, they go elsewhere, often leaving the child care field.

Look for special licensing. The best known is the NAEYC (National Association for the Education of Young Children), which has a multifaceted approach. Centers spend several months doing self-assessments and correcting any weak areas; they then are visited by independent accreditors, usually on several occasions. This accreditation is only valid for two years, then must be repeated. Programs displaying this type of accreditation truly have earned it.

The Staff

Training and experience make it more likely that caregivers will truly understand the needs of young children, provide activities that meet those needs, and have developmentally appropriate expectations. Some studies report that when child care providers complete training, they give more sensitive and appropriate care. Education added to low turnover indicates experienced caregivers, a winning situation for everyone involved.

Look for the types of training staff members receive. Are there special training requirements? Montessori and Waldorf programs have specialized training curriculum for their teachers. Community college, undergraduate, and master's level degree programs in early childhood studies exist in every state. Do staff members stay current by taking part in seminars, workshops, and special-topic training such as Positive Discipline? Does the licensing board require continuing education on a regular basis?

Look for harmony. When there is discord at a center, the children feel it. Remember, young children can read the energy of the adults around them and they respond to what they sense. Centers that encourage cooperation—between children and staff members—model the value of teamwork. Look for regularly scheduled staff meetings, in-house communication tools, and camaraderie among staff members.

Doctors, stock market analysts, child care teachers—all must stay knowledgeable about current information in their fields. Do staff members at the center you're considering attend workshops? Are there in-house training programs, or are employees encouraged to take part in additional educational programs? Teachers learn about new research, get inspired by and reminded of basic concepts, or feel encouraged when they hear others share solutions to common dilemmas.

Discipline

Is there a written discipline policy? In what manner are problems handled? Are there texts on discipline recommended by the center? Ask what teachers do about a child who hits, bites, or grabs toys. Find out if teachers receive any training in how to deal with problems that arise. Does the center condone spanking? Is the attitude at the center positive or punitive? Are children being shown what to do more often than being reprimanded about what not to do?

Watch how teachers talk with children:

- Does the teacher get down to the child's eye level when talking to him or do teachers just holler instructions across the room?

- Do teachers speak to children in a respectful way?

- Are boundaries made clear or does a teacher giggle uncomfortably when children run up and slam into her?

- Do teachers follow through? For instance, does a teacher call out to a child to "Put down that stick!" and then proceed to chat with a coworker while the child brandishes the stick overhead? Or does the teacher walk over and calmly remove the stick after giving the child a moment or two to do so himself?

Remember, the best child care emphasizes respect, kindness and firmness, and encouragement—just as you do at home.

Consistency

Consistency in the curriculum means that certain activities are provided regularly. Show and tell, daily story time, and singing are examples. Children thrive on routine—at their care facility as well as at home. Consistency also means that learning objectives exist and are implemented. Contrast a well-defined program to a place where children are given some old egg cartons to cut up, plopped down in front of the same container of blocks every morning, or left to watch endless videos and television programs. In the context of a clear curriculum, some of these activities may be fine. Just be sure that the program values hands-on learning, healthy activity, and developmental growth—not just silence and obedience.

Is there consistency from teacher to teacher or class to class in the way problems are handled? Does one teacher refuse to allow children to help prepare snacks while another turns snack time into a yogurt finger painting free-for-all?

Centers with consistent programs encourage children to develop trust, initiative, and a healthy sense of autonomy. If these tasks are important at home, they must also be important where your child will spend so much of his time. Consistency begins with center management.

- Are expectations made clear?
- Are events well organized?
- Do finances get handled in a businesslike manner?

Safety

Safety includes the physical setting, the program health policies, and the emergency preparedness of the center. A program with exposed electrical cords, unimpeded access to a laundry cupboard, or broken-down play equipment does not provide an environment safe for little ones. Leaving a tiny child in the care of other people each day requires faith.

Watching the way a teacher sprays the changing table with bleach solution after every diaper change reassures a watching parent that her son will not be exposed to dangerous bacteria. Seeing the center staff load the blocks into the dishwasher each evening gives Marnie peace of mind when she sees her toddler handling those same blocks the following morning. Mr. and Mrs. Jamison visit their daughter's center and see the staff and children participating in a fire drill. They are impressed with the level of competence shown at the center—and it even gets them thinking about the need to develop their own evacuation plan at home.

Find out if staff members have current CPR and first-aid training and HIV/AIDS training. Under what conditions will sick children be sent home? Look for fire safety procedures and earthquake or other emergency preparedness. Ask how injuries are handled. Reassure yourself that the adults in this place know how to care for your child under a variety of circumstances.

Trust Yourself—and Get Involved!

ONLY YOU CAN decide what your needs as a family really are. If you decide there is a need for outside care, use the guidelines listed above to find the best possible place to entrust the care of your little one. Be sure to stay involved and tuned in; if at all possible, make occasional visits to the child care center to reassure yourself that all is well.

No center or staff is ever perfect. If there are changes or improvements you would like to see made at your center or day care home, work toward bringing them about, support your program's efforts, and recognize the caregivers as a valuable extended family, part of your child-rearing team. Above all, give up your guilt button. Whether you care for your infant or toddler at home or entrust her to a child care center, you are likely to have some mixed emotions. Pay attention, make choices as wisely as you can, then relax and trust your choice. We are all in the same boat when it comes to raising our children. All children will inherit this earth—no matter where they took their naps, got cuddled, or first discovered *Curious George.* Knowledge and awareness will help us give our children everything they need during their important first three years of life.

If there are changes or improvements you would like to see made at your center or day care home, work toward bringing them about, support your program's efforts, and recognize the caregivers as a valuable extended family, part of your child-rearing team.

18

Building a Safety Net

Finding Support, Resources, and Sanity

N O MATTER HOW sweet-tempered your new babe and no matter how delighted you are to be a parent, these first months and years can be a very lonely experience. For mothers (or fathers) staying at home with a new baby, the demands of the job can be tough. Long nights punctuated by endless feedings and diaper changes numb even the most devoted mom or dad. A spouse or partner may find blow-by-blow descriptions of your baby's bowel movements enthralling, but many people will not. After a while, most parents long for a real adult conversation.

Many parents are tempted to blurt out, "Talk to me!" to anyone who wanders by, and with good reason. It is essential for new parents to seek out support through the early weeks and months of parenting. Connection with other adults nourishes new parents and, through them, their children and families.

Learning from the Wisdom of Others

WHILE PEOPLE SELDOM agree on every detail of raising infants and children, building a support network, a circle of friends who've been there, provides an invaluable source of information about raising and living with children.

It can be helpful to have people to call when things happen that you weren't expecting. Make an effort to build relationships with folks who have children the same age as yours—or who have recently survived the stage you're going through. Don't be afraid to ask lots of questions; finding out that other people's children have done the same strange or appalling things can make you feel normal again!

Some options include church or community-based mom and tot groups, community college parent-tot classes, and simple friendships with neighboring moms. One successful model is PEPS, a community-based program that began in the Northwest. "Save the Children Canada" now uses the PEPS program throughout the country. PEPS groups form right after a baby's birth and consist of people whose babies are born within days or weeks of one another. These families meet regularly in each other's homes or in family centers. There is also a special program for teen parents. The goal is to reduce isolation and create a network of support, resources, and encouragement. (PEPS, the Program for Early Parent Support, can be contacted at 206-547-8570 or *pepsgroup@aol.com*. Replication kits are available. PEPS is a United Way–affiliated agency.) Look for similar programs in your area, or consider initiating one of your own.

If you live in an isolated area or have no new moms nearby, the magic of the Internet offers chat groups, question-and-answer boards, and lots of general information. One such resource is *www.momsonline.com,* which is an interactive parenting magazine offering resources on Positive Discipline information, other special topics, and parenting chat rooms. Or you can receive information about Positive Discipline directly at *www.positivediscipline.com.* Even without home computer access, such services are available at local libraries. Ask a librarian or computer-literate friend to help you do a search for parenting resources; you'll be astonished at what you discover.

Still, there's nothing like real, live people. If you can, find a parenting group for parents of young children. Perhaps your parenting group, with dinner out beforehand, can be part of your special time with your partner. However you arrange it, having a sympathetic group with whom to discuss problems, ask questions, and explore the mysteries of raising very young children can make all the difference in the world. Consult your pediatrician, too. Family doctors see and hear a great deal as they go about the business of helping young patients and parents. They can often provide support as well as practical information and advice.

No matter where you find support, however, remember that in the end you must decide what feels right for you and your child. Gather all the wisdom and advice you can, then listen to your heart before you choose what will work best for you.

> No matter where you find support, however, remember that in the end you must decide what feels right for you and your child. Gather all the wisdom and advice you can, then listen to your heart before you choose what will work best for you.

Refilling the Pitcher

Q. *Oh, gosh, where do I start? I had no intention of writing anyone, but after thinking about my own parenting challenges, I'm all misty-eyed. I am a young mother with three children who are younger than five years of age. They are my greatest joy and I dearly love being a mother! Lately, though, I'm really overwhelmed. My husband works long hours and attends evening school. I do the housekeeping, work* *part-time, pay the bills, take care of business, and raise the children. They are smart, nice, talented kids (I'm a little subjective, of course!), but they are all, more or less, what you call strong-willed children. I feel like I'm pulled in so many directions, and no matter what I do, it's never enough.*

From the minute I wake up until late at night (it's already 11:42 P.M.), I never get more than a minute to myself. I'm so busy; I just have to smile wryly to myself when mothers of just one or two complain! I'm always tired and sick, and I get terrible headaches. The bottom line is that I've been losing my temper a lot lately. Then I'm even more upset because I feel so guilty. I've read so many books and magazines, and I understand and agree with Positive Discipline in theory. No offense, but usually the examples and ideas seem so far removed from my real life *that it just makes me more depressed. Maybe I just needed to vent a little. Thanks, A Very Tired Mom*

A. We know that words are inadequate when you are "in the trenches." You are not working part-time or even full-time, but overtime! No one flies around wearing a supermom cape. We stumble sometimes, doing the best we can and wondering if it's enough.

What's wrong with the picture you describe? The person you are not taking care of is you—and everyone suffers because of it. It is easy to get so busy with all of life's have-to's that our own needs get shoved not only to the back burner but completely off the stove. The best thing you can give to your family is a calm, rested you.

> The best thing you can give to your family is a calm, rested you.

Consider getting a high school student to help with the housework. Be creative if money is short; perhaps you can barter something. Trade baby-sitting hours with someone else so you can go for a walk, take a yoga class, or get in a swim and sauna at the local Y once or twice a week. Your family will notice the difference, and of course so will you.

Being a parent is a great deal like pouring water from a pitcher: you can only pour out so many glasses without refilling the pitcher. All too often, parents and other caregivers suddenly realize they've poured themselves dry for their children—the pitcher is empty. Effective, loving parenting takes a lot of time and energy. You can't do your best when your pitcher is empty, when you're tired, cranky, stressed out, and overwhelmed. How do you refill the pitcher? Taking care of yourself—filling up your pitcher before it runs dry—can take any form. If you find yourself daydreaming in a quiet moment about all the things you'd like to do, that may be a clue that you should consider ways to take care of yourself. Following are a few suggestions.

Budget Time Wisely

Most parents find that they must adjust their priorities after the arrival of a child. It can be extremely helpful—and quite a revelation—to keep track for a few days of exactly how you spend your time. Some activities, such as work, school, or tasks directly related

PARENT CARE

It is important to take care of yourself as well as you take care of your child. Our suggestions to prevent feeling overwhelmed are

- Budget time wisely.
- Make lists.
- Make time for important relationships.
- Do the things you enjoy.

to raising your children, can't be changed much. But we spend much of our time on activities other than our true priorities.

For instance, if you're often up during the night with an infant or very young child, make an effort to nap when your child naps. It is tempting to fly around the house doing all that "should" get done, but cleaning the bathroom and dusting the furniture will wait for you; you'll be a happier and more effective person if you get enough sleep.

Time is precious and all too short when you share your life with young children; be sure you're spending the time you do have as wisely as you can.

Make Lists

In a quiet moment, list all the things you'd like to do (or wish you could get around to). Then, when your child is napping or with a caregiver, spend those precious hours working your way down your list. Be sure you include not just chores and duties but activities that nurture you, like curling up with a good book, soaking in the tub, or having a cozy telephone chat with a friend.

Make Time for Important Relationships

It's amazing how therapeutic a simple cup of tea with a good friend can be, and sometimes a vigorous game of racquetball can restore a positive perspective on life. Conversation with caring adults can refresh you, especially when your world is populated with energetic little people. You and your partner may trade time watching the children so each of you has time for friends, or you may choose to spend special time together with other couples whose company you enjoy. Meeting friends at the park can give both adults and children time to rest and relax together. Keeping your world wide enough to include people outside your family can help you retain your health and balance.

Do the Things You Enjoy

It is important that you find time for the things that make you feel alive and happy, whether it's riding your bicycle, playing softball, singing with a choir, tinkering with machinery, working in the garden, or designing a quilt. Hobbies and exercise are important for your mental and emotional health—and you'll be a far more patient and effective parent if you're investing time and energy in your own well-being. Yes, finding time for these things can be a problem, and it is tempting to tell yourself, "I'll get around to that later." All too often, though, "later" never arrives. Even twenty minutes a day for something you love is a good beginning. Trust us: your children will survive. In fact, they'll thrive all the more with healthy, well-supported parents.

> Hobbies and exercise are important for your mental and emotional health—and you'll be a far more patient and effective parent if you're investing time and energy in your own well-being.

Learning to Recognize— and Manage—Stress

CLENCHED TEETH AND fists, tight muscles, headaches, a sudden desire to burst into tears or lock yourself in the bathroom—these are the symptoms of parental stress and overload; it's important to pay attention to them. Most parents—especially first-time parents—occasionally feel overwhelmed and exhausted and even angry or resentful. Because we want so much to be "good" parents, we may find it difficult to discuss these troubling thoughts and feelings with others.

Kim Parker had just managed to fall asleep when it started: the fretful, whining cry that told her that two-month-old Betsy was awake—

again. Kim groaned, thought briefly about burying her head under her pillow, then heaved herself out of bed. Her husband had been out of town on business for more than a week, and this was the second time tonight that Betsy had awakened. Kim was exhausted.

She stumbled into the baby's room and began her night routine without even bothering to turn on the light. Half an hour later, Betsy had been fed, changed, and burped, but she was crying more loudly than ever. Kim settled the baby in her arms and began rocking in the old rocking chair, fighting the urge to cry herself. She felt helpless, completely at the mercy of this tiny person who couldn't even tell her what was wrong. She hadn't had time to do the laundry in a week, the house was cluttered, and she would have given her right arm for an hour at the hairdresser's. What had happened? This wasn't what she'd imagined when she was pregnant with Betsy.

Kim looked down at her daughter's face and suddenly saw not a beautiful, beloved baby, but an ugly, demanding, noisy monster who wouldn't even let her get a decent night's sleep. What Kim really wanted was to put the baby down and simply leave.

It took almost two hours, but Betsy, soothed by the steady rocking, eventually fell asleep. It took her horrified mother a lot longer to deal with the unexpectedly strong emotions the encounter had created in her.

As we've mentioned before, there's a difference between a feeling and an action. It's not unusual for parents of infants and young children to be frustrated, overwhelmed, and exhausted, and most parents feel terribly guilty for feeling anger and resentment toward their children. The feelings are quite normal—but we need to be careful what we do with them.

If you find yourself struggling with anger or resentment or wanting to snap or lash out at your children, accept those feelings as your cue to do something to care for yourself. Make sure your children are safely occupied and take a few minutes of time-out (it usually works better for parents than for kids). Better yet, arrange for some time to do something to nurture yourself. Exhaustion and frustration can lead even the best parents to say and do things they later regret; it's far better to invest the time it takes to help yourself feel better.

Emergency Relief

IN THE EVENT you feel completely unable to cope, do not hesitate to seek help. Most communities offer a crisis line for immediate phone assistance. Some hospitals provide similar services; a few moments speaking to an understanding, reassuring adult may make a world of difference.

If you ever feel your child might be at risk, check to see if respite care is available in your community. It is not wrong or shameful to need help; it is true wisdom to ask for it.

> If you find yourself struggling with anger or resentment or wanting to snap or lash out at your children, accept those feelings as your cue to do something to care for yourself.

If Your Child Has Special Needs

EVERY NEW PARENT counts toes and fingers and worries about anything that seems wrong. Sadly, sometimes these worries are founded. If you have concerns, take them seriously and ask your pediatrician or community health nurse to check them out. Identifying a child's special needs early promises the best results.

Rosemary noticed that her four-month-old daughter did not wave at her crib mobile the way her friend's son did. She also thought her daughter, Angela, seemed to turn her eyes inward at times. At first, Rosemary told herself she was imagining things. Then she decided to have Angela's eyes checked at the local clinic, just for her own peace of mind. Even if something was wrong, Rosemary doubted that it was possible to treat an infant's eyes. To her surprise, Angela was diagnosed with strabismus, or crossed eyes, and within two weeks was fitted with special, tiny eyeglasses.

This early intervention probably saved Angela's vision. Untreated, crossed eyes can result in a loss of vision in one of the eyes, but early intervention prevented that from happening. Angela, now in grade school, sees beautifully and no longer needs glasses of any kind.

Speech, hearing, and vision problems are all common in very young children. These problems can and should be treated as soon as possible. A child with frequent ear infections does not hear sounds consistently, and his developing speech patterns may suffer. If you are unable to understand a child at all by the age of two and a half, consider getting a speech evaluation from a qualified speech therapist. Early speech therapy often provides excellent results.

The teachers at Aaron's preschool were frustrated. He did not seem to listen to them at all. One day his teacher tried an experiment. She stood behind Aaron, out of sight and rang a small bell. All the other children turned in her direction. Aaron did not. Then she whispered his name. Again there was no response. The teacher urged Aaron's mom to seek a hearing evaluation. As it turned out, Aaron had a partial hearing loss. He received treatment, and his teachers learned to make eye contact before speaking to him. Not surprisingly, his behavior improved at once.

One advantage of early programs for young children are routine screenings by public health nurses or other community or school personnel. Whatever the concern, parents need to trust their own instincts and seek help when worried about a child's health or development. The possibility of their child being less than perfect terrifies most parents. Early diagnosis and intervention will help you and your child feel better.

The possibility of their child being less than perfect terrifies most parents. Early diagnosis and intervention will help you and your child feel better.

Reach Out and Touch Someone

BETH LOOKED BACK *at the front window, where her friend Caroline held fourteen-month-old Gregory up to wave good-bye. As she slipped behind the wheel of the minivan, Beth looked at the two good friends who shared the back seat.*

SHARING THE ATTENTION

Q. I have three boys. My oldest turns six in March, the next will be four in February, and my youngest just turned two. The oldest and youngest of my boys are profoundly deaf. My problem, however, lies with my middle child. He is a very bright child who has been sandwiched between two siblings who require special attention. As a result he has taken on responsibilities beyond his age.

In the last month, however, we have noticed him becoming defiant. He whines all the time now when he doesn't get his way, and he has become somewhat withdrawn. This is totally the opposite of his personality just a month ago. I have racked my brain trying to find out what is different in our lives, daily routines, or anything that would account for this change. I know he receives a different type of attention than his brothers, but he does not receive any less attention.

Is there something I'm missing? Do you have any suggestions? Or is this just a phase and it too shall pass? Please, any ideas would be greatly appreciated.

A. It takes a great deal of patience and sensitivity to raise children with special needs, particularly when you have more than one. We know that children are wonderful perceivers but not very good interpreters, and children often believe that the special therapies, doctor's appointments, and treatment that their special-needs siblings receive indicate more parental love and attention. Attention isn't just a matter of quantity—it's a matter of the beliefs and feelings that children form about how much they (and their siblings) receive and what that tells them about their special place in the family.

"Boy, am I ready for this," she said.

Anne and Joleen laughed. "Us, too!" Joleen said. "And you'd better enjoy yourself—next week, the kids are all at your place."

Beth, Anne, Joleen, and Caroline had been sharing their "moms' day out" for about six months, and none could imagine how they'd survived without it. Each Saturday morning, one of the four women cared for the

It's also wise to remember that while children develop at different paces emotionally as well as physically, three-year-olds are often experimenting with what we call "initiative"—forming their own plans, wanting to do things their own way and, occasionally, practicing that by becoming defiant, whining, and so on.

You're probably right that some of this will pass, but here are some suggestions to try in the meantime:

- If you don't already have them, create routines for morning, evening, off to school, and so on. Each child can have special tasks that he performs, and once the routine is in place (a big chart can help), the routine becomes the "boss." It's wonderful that your middle son wants to help and be responsible, but children sometimes make themselves overesponsible in an effort to earn love and belonging. Because your son is bright and all children are naturally egocentric at that age, he may feel responsible somehow for being the only hearing child in his family; he may feel guilty for being able to hear. Make sure he knows it's okay just to be a kid and that his brothers' deafness is not about him.

- It may help to set aside special time with each child, time that you spend just with him. This doesn't mean spending money or huge chunks of time—fifteen minutes to go for a walk, throw the ball, or to read a story is usually all it takes. During your special time, ask your middle son to share his happiest and saddest times of the day; be prepared to listen well and to share your own. The keys to his behavior lie in what he believes about himself and his place in the family.

group's six children. Lunches were packed, activities were planned—and the three moms who had the day off had four blissful hours to shop, play golf, take a walk, or just share conversation and a cup of coffee. All had felt a bit guilty at first, but they quickly learned to wave bye-bye and drive away, knowing their children were well cared for—and would be happy to have a calm, cheerful mother pick them up. Because the women were careful always to return at the designated time, no one felt taken advantage of.

Support comes packaged in different ways. Whatever works for you and wherever you find it, accept it with gratitude. Parenting is too big a job to tackle alone. Children and their families need a community of support. The face that community wears may be that of a familiar relative, a parenting class, good friends, or even words floating through cyberspace. The important thing is that it is there. Use it—for everyone's sake.

CONCLUSION

THERE IS AN old song whose lyrics go something like this:

"Where are you going, my little one, little one,
Where are you going, my baby, my own,
Turn around, and you're two,
Turn around, and you're four,
Turn around, and you're a young man
Walking out of the door . . ."

It sometimes seems as though the first three years last forever. We live with the endless succession of diapers and bottles—and, sometimes, the equally endless nights—and we can hardly wait to get on to the next stage of our child's life.

And so we enter the toddler years. We rush around childproofing our home, trying to remain calm and patient, doing our best to cope with our active, challenging little person and his occasional tantrums and misbehaviors. We collapse, exhausted, at the end of another hectic day—and we can hardly wait to get on to the next stage of our child's life.

And so it goes. Ask parents whose children are older, whose children are busy with school and friends, whose children are independent teenagers, or whose children have grown up and begun a family of their own, and they will tell you: the first three years go by too fast, far more quickly than we can know when we're in the midst of them.

In only an instant, the darling little outfits will have been outgrown, the binkies and blankies cast aside. The favorite toys will lie untouched in the closet while their formerly devoted owner busies himself with new activities and new friends. It may be incomprehensible now, but the day will come when you watch your confident, eager child run to meet his friends and find yourself longing for exactly what you have now: the sweet, cuddly baby who needs you so desperately, the busy toddler who can turn your world upside down and still capture your heart with a single glance, the young child who tests your patience and perseverance one moment, then runs to hug you and plant a sticky kiss on your cheek the next.

There is a great deal to learn and remember when you're raising a young child. We ponder feeding schedules, toilet training, eating habits, and various methods of discipline. We wonder if we're competent enough, loving enough, or just plain good enough at this awesome task. Often we parents get caught up in our responsibilities and duties, and we certainly do have many of them, all important. Sometimes we long for peace, quiet, and time to ourselves.

But if there's one lesson we, as authors and as parents of children now well beyond their first three years, would want to share with you, it is this: cherish these moments while they are yours. Stop to wonder at the miracle of a sleeping infant, the marvel of a curious toddler. Take a slow, deep breath and savor the joy of watching your child learn, grow, and discover his place in this world. Take lots of photographs; make time to laugh, to play, to simply enjoy. These first years will be gone before you know it.

It is our hope as authors that in these pages you have found information you can use as you and your little one navigate these critical first months and years together. It is a vitally important time; both of you are learning a lot, and both of you will make lots of mistakes. Remember that mistakes are merely opportunities to learn and grow together and that the hugs and tears that sometimes follow mistakes may actually draw you closer to those you love.

The best gifts we have to offer our children are not things they can touch, hold, or play with. In fact, they may not recognize or appreciate these gifts for years yet. They are, nonetheless, priceless. We can offer our children trust, dignity, and respect. We can believe in them, encourage them, and teach them. We can bestow on them the gifts of confidence, responsibility, and competence. And we can show them how to love and appreciate life by sharing it with them, every step of the way.

Learn as much as you can; ask for help when you need it. Watch, listen, and learn to understand the child you have. Most important of all, have the courage to trust your own wisdom and knowledge of your child. There is no greater challenge than parenting—and no job more rewarding.

SELECT BIBLIOGRAPHY

Adler, Alfred. *Understanding Human Nature.* Translated by W. Beran Wolfe. Greenwich, CT: Fawcett Publications Inc., 1954.

Chess, Stella, M.D., and Alexander Thomas, M.D. *Know Your Child.* New York: Basic Books, 1987.

Dreikurs, Rudolf. *Fundamentals of Adlerian Psychology.* Chicago: Alfred Adler Institute, 1953.

Erikson, Erik H. *Childhood and Society.* New York: Norton, 1963.

Ferber, Richard. *Solve Your Child's Sleep Problems.* New York: Fireside Books, 1985.

Glenn, H. Stephen, and Jane Nelsen. *Raising Self-Reliant Children in a Self-Indulgent World.* Rocklin, CA: Prima Publishing, 1989.

Harlow, Harry F. *Learning to Love.* New York: Ballantine, 1971.

Healy, Jane M. *Endangered Minds: Why Children Don't Think and What We Can Do About It.* New York: Simon & Schuster, 1990.

Munsch, Robert, and Sheila McGraw. *Love You Forever.* Willowdale, Ontario, Canada: Firefly Books Ltd., 1986.

Nelsen, Jane. *Positive Discipline.* New York: Ballantine, 1996.

Nelsen, Jane; Cheryl Erwin; and Carol Delzer. *Positive Discipline for Single Parents.* Rocklin, CA: Prima Publishing, 1994.

Nelsen, Jane; Cheryl Erwin; and Roslyn Duffy. *Positive Discipline for Preschoolers.* Rocklin, CA: Prima Publishing, 1998.

Nelsen, Jane; Riki Intner; and Lynn Lott. *Positive Discipline for Parenting in Recovery.* Rocklin, CA: Prima Publishing, 1996.

Nelsen, Jane; Lynn Lott; and H. Stephen Glenn. *Positive Discipline A–Z.* Rocklin, CA: Prima Publishing, 1993.

Piaget, Jean. *The Origins of Intelligence in Children.* New York: International Universities Press, 1952.

Sammons, William. *The Self-Calmed Baby.* New York: Little, Brown, 1989.

Shore, Rima. *Rethinking the Brain: Research and Implications of Brain Development in Young Children.* New York: Families and Work Institute, 1997.

INDEX

The Ultimate Parenting Encyclopedia

Wouldn't it be nice if there was a book that listed in alphabetical order every child-raising problem parents could imagine? Here it is—from bestselling parenting experts Jane Nelsen, Lynn Lott, and H. Stephen Glenn. This book not only helps parents solve problem behavior, but also helps children feel good about themselves, gain self-confidence and self-discipline, learn responsibility, and develop problem-solving skills.

- **What should I do when she has a temper tantrum in the grocery store?**
- **What should I do when he won't eat his dinner?**
- **What should I do when she won't go to bed at night?**

ISBN 0-7615-1470-8 / Paperback / 352 pages
U.S. $16.95 / Can. $25.95

The Partner Every Single Parent Needs

Being a single parent in this complex world of ours can be both an overwhelming and exhilarating challenge. In *Positive Discipline for Single Parents,* the authors emphasize ways in which single parents can make clear, focused discipline decisions while maintaining positive levels of interaction with their children. Learn how to:

- **Redefine the parenting role**
- **Set the stage for teamwork**
- **Deal with feelings and emotions**
- **Balance your priorities**
- **Understand misbehavior**
- **Create a partnership with your child**

The authors also provide reassuring answers to questions about your social life, your children's emotional stability, and other pertinent questions that plague parents from time to time.

ISBN 0-7615-2011-2 / Paperback / 272 pages
U.S. $16.95 / Can. $25.95

Available everywhere books are sold.
Visit us online at www.randomhouse.com.

For Teachers and Parents

Positive Discipline in the Classroom, Revised 3rd Edition, addresses the popular concept of class meetings, where students and teachers discuss moral, ethical, and behavioral issues and work together to solve problems. Students learn a number of social skills through the class-meeting process, such as how to listen, take turns, hear different points of view, negotiate, and communicate. This book covers:

- **Building blocks for successful class meetings**
- **Effective problem-solving skills**
- **Classroom management skills**
- **And so much more!**

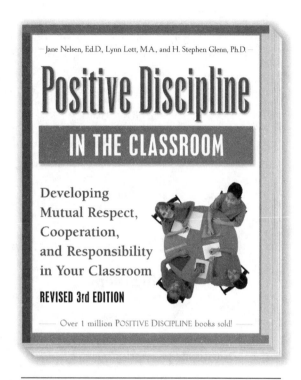

ISBN 0-7615-2421-5 / Paperback / 272 pages
U.S. $16.95 / Can. $25.95

FOR MORE INFORMATION

Workshops, seminars, and facilitator trainings are scheduled throughout the United States each year. Workshops include:

Teaching Parenting the Positive Discipline Way
(a two-day workshop for parent educators)

Positive Discipline for Parents
(a one-day workshop)

Positive Discipline in the Classroom
(a one-day or two-day workshop for teachers and school personnel)

Dates and locations are available by contacting:

Empowering People
P.O. Box 1926
Orem, UT 84059-1926
1-800-456-7770
E-mail: JaneNelsen@aol.com
Web Site: www.positivediscipline.com

The authors also provide dynamic lectures, seminars, and conference keynote presentations. For more information or to schedule a presentation, call 1-800-456-7770.

ORDER FORM

To: Empowering People, P.O. Box 1926, Orem, UT 84059-1926
Phone: 1-800-456-7770 (credit card orders only)
Fax: 801-762-0022
Web Site: www.positivediscipline.com for discount prices

BOOKS

	Price	Quantity	Amount
Positive Discipline for Your Stepfamily, by Nelsen, Erwin, & Glenn	$16.95	_____	_____
Positive Discipline for Single Parents, by Nelsen, Erwin, & Delzer	$16.95	_____	_____
Positive Discipline in the Classroom, by Nelsen, Lott, & Glenn	$16.95	_____	_____
Positive Discipline: A Teacher's A–Z Guide, by Nelsen, Duffy, Escobar, Ortolano, & Owen-Sohocki	$16.95	_____	_____
Positive Discipline for Preschoolers, by Nelsen, Erwin, & Duffy	$16.95	_____	_____
Positive Discipline: The First Three Years, by Nelsen, Erwin, & Duffy	$16.95	_____	_____
Positive Discipline, by Nelsen	$12.00	_____	_____
Positive Discipline A–Z, by Nelsen, Lott, & Glenn	$16.95	_____	_____
Positive Discipline for Teenagers, by Nelsen & Lott	$16.95	_____	_____
Positive Discipline for Parenting in Recovery, by Nelsen, Intner, & Lott	$12.95	_____	_____
Raising Self-Reliant Children in a Self-Indulgent World, by Glenn & Nelsen	$15.95	_____	_____
Positive Time-Out: And 50 Other Ways to Avoid Power Struggles, Nelsen	$12.95	_____	_____
From Here to Serenity, by Nelsen	$14.00	_____	_____
Positive Discipline in the Christian Home, by Nelsen, Erwin, Brock & Hughes	$16.95	_____	_____
Positive Discipline for Childcare Providers, by Nelsen & Erwin	$16.95	_____	_____

MANUALS

Teaching Parenting the Positive Discipline Way, by Lott & Nelsen	$49.95	_____	_____
Positive Discipline in the Classroom, by Nelsen & Lott	$49.95	_____	_____

TAPES AND VIDEOS

Positive Discipline audiotape	$10.00	_____	_____
Positive Discipline videotape	$49.95	_____	_____
Building Healthy Self-Esteem Through Positive Discipline audiotape	$10.00	_____	_____

SUBTOTAL _____

Sales tax: UT add 6.25%; CA add 7.25% _____

Shipping & handling: $3.00 plus $0.50 each item _____

(Prices subject to change without notice.) **TOTAL** _____

METHOD OF PAYMENT (check one):
_____ Check made payable to Empowering People Books, Tapes, & Videos
_____ MasterCard, Visa, Discover Card, American Express

Card # _____ Expiration _____ / _____

Ship to _____

Address _____

City/State/Zip _____

Daytime phone (_____)_____

ABOUT THE AUTHORS

 **Jane Nelsen** is a popular lecturer and co-author of the entire POSITIVE DISCIPLINE series. She has appeared on *Oprah* and *Sally Jesse Raphael* and was the featured parent expert on the "National Parent Quiz" hosted by Ben Vereen. Jane is the mother of seven children and the grandmother of sixteen.

 **Cheryl Erwin** is a marriage and family therapist in private practice. For the past nine years she has also been a consultant, writer, and speaker on parenting issues. Cheryl lives with her husband and fourteen-year-old son in Reno, Nevada.

 **Roslyn Duffy** cofounded and directed the Learning Tree Montessori Child Care. She currently directs the Better Living Institute, maintains a private counseling practice, conducts parent and teacher training programs, and appears as a featured speaker in person, on local National Public Radio, and on *MomsOnline* Internet magazine. Her column, "From a Parent's Perspective," appears in *Child Care Information Exchange* magazine. Roslyn lives in Seattle, Washington, with her husband and four children.